HAUNTED WATERBURY & THE NAUGATUCK VALLEY

HAUNTED WATERBURY & THE NAUGATUCK VALLEY

MICHAEL J. BIELAWA

Haunted America

Published by Haunted America
A division of The History Press
An imprint of Arcadia Publishing
Charleston, SC
www.historypress.com

First published 2025

Manufactured in the United States

ISBN 9781467159012

Library of Congress Control Number: 2025937579

*To all the rivers and roads that carry our memories and always bring us home…
and to my grandparents, who first mapped these places in my heart: the Mohawk,
Chucktanunda, Housatonic, Route 8 and the backwoods Berkshire lanes…
pathways that directed me to eventually seek the Naugatuck and its many
mysteries swirling inside this book. Thank you.*

CONTENTS

Acknowledgements 9
Introduction 13

PART I. PHANTASMA
1. Ghosts of Waterbury 19
 The Baldwin Street Demon House 19
 Quitting Time 23
 Evicted by a Ghost 24
 Disturber of Graves: When the City Hall Specter Calls 27
 The Last Library on the Left or, How Far the Mighty Fallen Fell 30
 Bound with a Dream: The Second Life of Lulu Morden 35

2. House of Thorn and Echo:
 Rose Hill Cottage (Waterbury) 41

3. Who Knocks? (Ansonia) 58

4. The Midnight Watchman (Ansonia) 64

5. Tales of the Bloody Hookman (Seymour) 72

6. Occurrences in the Birmingham National Bank:
 A Tale of Two Vaults (Derby) 78

Contents

Part II. Genii Locorum

7. Inside the Naugatuck Valley Vortex:
Strange Sights Overhead (Waterbury, Winsted) 95

8. The Kinneytown Entity (Seymour) 103
Walking Distance: Escaping the Kinneytown Entity 109

9. Seymour's Empty Sepulcher Sings a Silent Chantey (Seymour) 111

10. Something Wicked Slithers in Purgatory:
The Watertown Wyrm (Watertown) 124

11. The Devil's Address (Seymour-Oxford) 135

Part III. Omen Antiquitatum

12. The Summoning (Derby) 143

13. Living Apparitions:
A Doppelgänger's Forewarning (Ansonia-Derby) 146

Notes 151
About the Author 175

ACKNOWLEDGEMENTS

In 1992 when I first moved to the Naugatuck Valley, I was drawn to the marvelous Ansonia Public Library. The library's historical collections are housed in an elegant Victorian wood-paneled room where one encounters the rich aroma of leatherbound books and that unique sensation of incunabula only bibliophiles can wholly relish. In this inspiring setting, I first located a folder containing information about a fascinating old-time New England vagabond: John Brennan, better known as Johnny O' the Woods. This file's brittle hand-typed pages transcribed a cache of century-old newspaper articles focusing on Brennan's wanderings; this discovery shouted out from the far distances of time that curious and unique stories might indeed swirl along the riverbank of my new home, the Naugatuck Valley. *Haunted Waterbury* was about to set sail on a thirty-year voyage.

Over the course of the ensuing decades, I encountered many knowledgeable individuals keen on sharing their own paranormal experiences as well as all those who contributed to moving this project forward in myriad ways.

I'd like to recognize the staff and acknowledge the valuable collections housed in the Ansonia Public Library, Beacon Falls Public Library, Connecticut State Library, Derby Neck Library, Derby Public Library, Naugatuck's Howard Whittemore Memorial Library, Plumb Memorial Library in Shelton, Seymour Public Library, Torrington Library, Watertown Library Association and Waterbury's Silas Bronson Library (whose erudite director, Raechel Guest, we will revisit in the notes section). I express my sincerest thanks to you all. Research, like gold, is where you find it. And working with the Denver Public Library staff was a golden experience.

Mark Sweeney deserves high praise alone for his dedication to our nation's collected history, but his personal attention to locating the images I requested is outstanding. Mark is the Principal Deputy Librarian of Congress (just knowing someone with a dazzling job title like this is impressive). Thanks to him for his individual assistance in tracking down the images that appear in this book.

All of the dedicated folks at the Seymour Town Hall deserve high marks. The 1902 Map of Seymour was made available to me with the kind assistance of Town Clerk Lianna McMurray and the wonderful "Queen of Gnomes," Assistant Town Clerk Veronica Hoffman.

The Naugatuck Valley has an exuberance of wonderful museums and historical societies. Researching the chapter on Rose Hill Cottage offered me the opportunity to work with special people intimately familiar with the beautiful and mysterious mansion: I'd like to thank Stephanie Crawford and Dr. Frances Martin, the archivist librarians from the Max R. Traurig Library and Archive at Waterbury's Mattatuck Museum, who helped locate invaluable photographs. The Greater Waterbury YMCA is a wonderful facility (as a matter of fact, their administrative offices are located in the Rose Hill annex). Thanks to the Chief Executive Officer Jim O'Rourke and Senior Director of Operations Mike Tedesco for sharing their time and knowledge about the Rose Hill mansion. Additional thanks to Mike T. for providing an especially insightful tour of the historic landmark and grounds.

Diane Ciba, curator of the Watertown History Museum, enthralled me with the evolution of name origins concerning Nova Scotia Hill and Purgatory in Litchfield County. Emma Q. Norden, the research librarian at the New Haven Museum, was kind enough to lend me the use of their collection and workspace.

The talented and dedicated folks at the *Waterbury Republican-American* must be spotlighted: Publisher William B. Pape II and Managing Editor Anne Karolyi allowed me permission to use the newspaper's photos. My late wife Janice, who worked in the Art Department there, loved the *Rep-Am*; she enjoyed the newspaper life and felt a kinship to everyone at the paper. Thanks for keeping me a part of the family.

While researching these chapters, I conducted some intriguingly surreal and startling interviews: Aly Butler, John R. Fogerty, Nicholas Howard, Mike Picone, David Harmon, Liliana Feliciano, Carolyn (Barth) DeLieto and Tony Trungadi. Thanks to them for sharing such emotionally charged supernatural experiences. Each of them re-created frightening and solemn moments within haunted woods, a poltergeist-filled restaurant, a night at Hookman's Cemetery and a heartfelt ghostly experience. Much appreciation for the invitation to peer beyond this world's doorways of perception.

Old friends Chaz and AJ, Phil, Ruth and Ashley, thanks for the airtime on the all-powerful WPLR-FM 99.1. I appreciate our years of canvassing Connecticut residents about all sorts of hauntings during the radio station's Halloween-season "Freak Week." The breadth of your far-reaching curiosity is surpassed only by the size of your hearts.

I'd like to express my gratitude to two eateries that became my special homes as well as my literary thinktanks while I was composing this book. The romantic New England coffeehouse, Mystic Depot Roasters in Mystic, Connecticut—Ian, Andrea, Ell and Ken, thanks for providing me an Edwardian salon and writing chamber in your beautiful Georgian Revival railroad station. Your venue is an anchor of friendship in a marvelous village of seafaring history. Steps away from the wafting aroma of your brewing coffee, trains may rumble ever eastward toward Boston and westward to New Haven, but your coffeehouse remains a steadfast bastion of tranquility and inspiration. Now for the Valley Diner in Derby, Connecticut, which deserves a round of resounding applause. Great restaurants preserve tradition. Greater restaurants create friendships. To all the cooks and kitchen crew and waitstaff, including witty artists Vlora, Katie and Ashley, who love Halloween; Laura, who tells a wicked scary story; scholarly Ahmet; deep-thinking Turkay; Maria; Aly; Edlira ("put the cell phone down"); the ever-engaging Czar Nicholas; Gladis and Daye; Jess with an "X"; Carly and Mel and Mert and Debbie (Let's Go Mets!); Catie Catwalk; Lucas; "Crayons" Lazaro; dancing Rigo; thoughtful Irene; Marlin of Japanese cherry blossoms; Yeimi; Yesenia; and Kevin the Dude ("you know what I'm saying"); philosophical and kindhearted owners John and Peter and Themi, for allowing me to plug in my laptop and travel to other dimensions (all while eating an omelet); and of course, my fellow Knights of the Counter: John, Peter, old Tony and young Tony, thank you for your camaraderie. (Note: this is the place where I chest-bumped total strangers when Pete Alonzo hit his ninth-inning home run that hurtled the New York Mets into the postseason.)

The earliest iterations of this ever-evolving manuscript became tactile and publisher-ready through the perseverance (and sense of humor) of my longtime friend Nancy Sweeney. You deserve a big-time thank-you!

Wow: Mary Iorio, thanks for endless hours of editing. And smiling the while! Editing and tolerating me. Matthew and Janet, you are the best at playing the fun game I invented—ceaseless sessions of "this or that" word selections. Soooo fun! I love you.

And finally, and as importantly, I want to acknowledge the editors at The History Press. Your guidance and especially your patience throughout this process have been invaluable.

If I have inadvertently missed mentioning anyone, please accept my apologies. Before the veil of haunted Waterbury is pulled aside, I want to express my deepest appreciation to everyone who helped make this book of the unreal a reality. I raise my midnight mug of diner coffee to you all.

INTRODUCTION

It is the thing mysterious, the thing profound, unknown, the country of mirage and of phantasmagoria, where one sees, at night, things which do not exist, where one hears strange noises, where one trembles causelessly, as though crossing a graveyard. And it is, indeed, the most sinister of graveyards—a graveyard where there are no tombstones.
—Guy De Maupassant, "On the River," 1876

At night, don't be found on the river road.

The Naugatuck Valley and its eponymous waterway cradle a murky and foreboding history. A paranormal legacy flows here with the meandering river's miasmatic mists. Hauntings, monsters, mystifying visions and inexplicable aerial phenomena have long plagued the banks (and skies) of the Naugatuck River. Where folks once physically shunned the supernatural sites herein discussed, over the decades, these surreal memories slowly washed away. It appeared that the river-worn tales vanished beneath the Naugatuck's chemically dyed currents. But one undiluted fact remains: legends cannot be drowned. And these ghosts, creatures and lurid mysteries, which never fully departed, have again been dragged to the surface of midnight consciousness with a historian's pen transformed into a grappling hook.

Commencing roughly 16,500 years ago, an Ice Age river carved a path through western Connecticut, obliterating and reshaping the landscape into something weird and stern. Today, this valley's namesake waterway flows approximately forty-five-plus miles, from its twin sources near Norfolk and Winchester toward Torrington. Here, the East and West Branches of the Naugatuck meet and then continue southward to its confluence with the Housatonic River in the old town of Birmingham, now Derby, Connecticut. The rolling river bears witness to an assortment of woodlands and rocky promontories, midsize cities and small towns. Much of the river's winding path is mirrored by nineteenth-century railroad tracks; these rails, some active but more often abandoned, lend themselves to the legacy of devastating overindustrialization.

The region's heavy industry, powered by the Naugatuck River, served as a devastating symbol of progress dating back to well before the American Civil War. The Naugatuck Valley encompassed a huge share of our nation's vital, and invincible, brass and copper manufacturers. The effect that this industry had on America cannot be downplayed. The metals created here in the Naugatuck Valley were dubbed by the *New York Times* the nineteenth-century equivalent of today's omnipresent plastic.

The Valley was also renowned for its chemical plants. Charles Goodyear first patented a formula for stabilizing rubber in the 1840s while living in the village of Naugatuck. There was a glaring and pervasive downside to this expanding industry. Some 120 years later, a person could still smell the hot mess. In addition to the sprawling brass mills and chemical sites, poisonous industrial waste, acid and raw sewage were ruthlessly pumped into the syrupy, polychromatic waterway. Nineteenth-century newspapers lamented how plagues of flies descended in biblical proportions on the stench of the Naugatuck River. Up to the waning decades of the twentieth century, during summer's steamiest days, drivers and passengers were compelled to roll up their windows and hold their breath while driving along long stretches of the Naugatuck Valley's Route 8 parallel to the Naugatuck River.

In his book *The Housatonic: Puritan River*, Chard Powers Smith offhandedly dismisses the Naugatuck as a "huge, nauseous, gray-green ribbon coiling out into the purer waters [of the Housatonic] and discoloring them for the rest of the journey to the sea." Smith woefully postulates, "Since the Naugatuck is entirely controlled by industry, all hope of curing this condition must be abandoned." Yes, abandon hope all ye who swim/boat/fish here.

It wasn't until the late 1970s and early 1980s that the valley's myriad foundries finally and forever recognized the death knell clanging from the green-patina bells they themselves forged. Employment numbers tumbled when the brass mills relocated. The effect on the local citizenry was sad, bitter and immediate. Over the next decade, the sprawling factories shuttered; these sooty-brick pillars of the community took on much of the same forlorn and defeated pathos as crumbling post–Civil War plantations but without the promise of Reconstruction. Jobs departed while the silent

Oh to Live on Tire Mountain… This April 1944 photograph taken at the Naugatuck Chemical Division Plant of the U.S. Rubber Co. shows the extent of industrialized sprawl that inundated the banks of the Naugatuck River. Once, this river (*pictured on the left*) flowed multicolored and choked with chemicals and poisons, but recent years have witnessed a return of abundant wildlife along this waterway where the river's ghosts never quite left. *Author's collection.*

smokestacks stayed. And of course, there was the river, in all its unnatural glory, rolling on abandoned as well. More than 150 years of gurgling toxicity had caused the Naugatuck to eventually be declared dead. Very dead. Dead with extreme prejudice.

In fact, as bizarre as it may seem, the destructive warfare between People versus Nature occurring within the Naugatuck Valley would one day be symbolically and dramatically reenacted on the river. In keeping with the Naugatuck's otherworldly legacy as described in this book, these brownfield-blasted shores would host an onslaught from the Red Planet: scenes from the Tom Cruise version of the classic sci-fi movie *The War of the Worlds* (2005) were filmed on the river's banks. At the movie's conclusion, Humankind triumphantly defeats the Martian war machines in a pitched battle taking place at the old Uniroyal Chemical Company's smokestacks mere feet from the Naugatuck's currents. But it wasn't a fictional Hollywood script that eventually rescued the Naugatuck River.

Around the same time that the very real-world's mills were closing, an ascendent environmental movement was afoot. Since the Nixon administration's environmental protections, positive actions began reversing the Naugatuck's post-industrial course. Public mood had changed, and anti-pollution laws were enacted. Nowadays, a casual visit to these banks provides glimpses of bald eagles, osprey and great blue herons. And more surprising yet, kayakers. Beautiful ornate stairs lead citizens to the meditative sounds of the babbling river. Naturalists and government officials have been creating a celebrated, and continually expanding, greenway along these reinvigorated shores. This trail provides an attractive setting for walking and biking. The transformation of the river is nothing less than astonishing.

Joining the resurrection of this beautiful natural world, a vastly different and darker realm roils to the river's surface. The Naugatuck, a waterway officially declared lifeless years ago, has actually very much risen from the dead. Yes, the swirling multicolored chemical monster has been eradicated—but different, perhaps more sinister, horrors remain.

All of the tales recounted in this work, according to eyewitness accounts and reports, are true. If they aren't, they should be. The weird documentation needed to create this book was synthesized over many years, gleaned from local newspaper collections housed in libraries up and down the Valley and found in the lower level of the Connecticut State Library. Stories were gathered during personal interviews and unearthed deep inside nineteenth-century town histories. These chapters fermented, bubbling and boiling, during long contemplations on the banks of the river itself. So many stories swirl here on the river that it seemed as though there was always one more chapter waiting around the next bend.

You now hold within your grasp the Naugatuck River's own gazetteer of the ghostly, a relumining of forbidden tales seemingly penned by Naugatuck naiads from within their watery lairs. Readers are implored to visit the Naugatuck Valley, roam the river towns, hike these New England woods, explore the back roads and cemeteries and stroll down the greenway's steps…take a moment to lean toward the river's *whispers*. Like the resuscitated Naugatuck River itself, these pages reanimate forgotten mysteries. But please, during your explorations, tarry only while sunlight remains. Remember, at night, don't be found on the river road.

Michael J. Bielawa
Ansonia, Connecticut
From the wooded banks above Coe Pond along the Naugatuck River
(Looking out on Route 8)

PART I
PHANTASMA

1

Ghosts of Waterbury

The Baldwin Street Demon House

What is now proved was once only imagined.
—William Blake, "The Marriage of Heaven and Hell," circa 1790

One wouldn't readily associate Connecticut's I-84 with the supernatural, especially where the elevated road's nondescript concrete and tar passes high above the Naugatuck River, but this convergence does indeed hold a strange place in the state's paranormal pantheon. The area where Interstate 84 crosses over the river and bisects Route 8 forms a crosshairs for the Brass City's spookiest sites. Just a short hop, skip and lithobolia stone's jump westward from the maze of exits and ramps called the Mixmaster, directly on the Middlebury border, there exists the mystical stone ruins known as the Village of the Little People. Looming to the east within sight of the interstate, the shambles of a long-abandoned roadside religious attraction called Holy Land broods somberly. But what drivers along this stretch of highway do not realize is that I-84 passes near one of Waterbury's most haunted grounds: the former setting of the Baldwin Street Demon House. A series of strange and inexplicable events occurred in this home—events that clawed at the minds of an entire city.

The apartment house at 16 Baldwin Street scowled on the neighborhood, just a short distance from where the old Scovill bridge linked with Bridge Street (to get an idea of the house's approximate location using present-

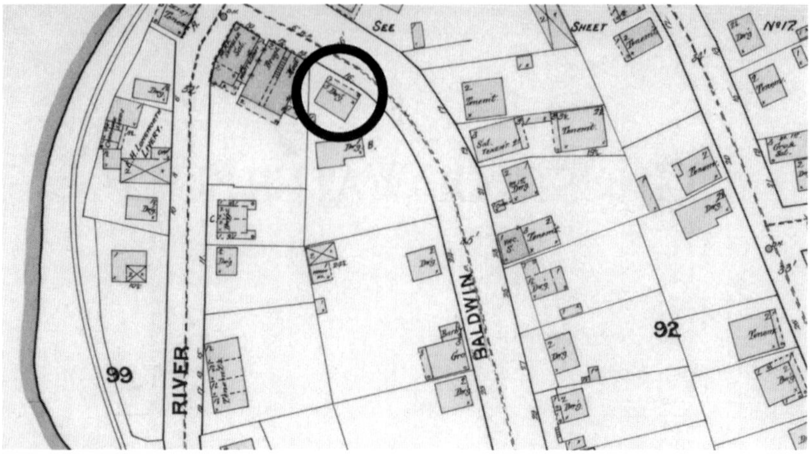

House of Demons. Horrific activity took place in this Waterbury apartment house during 1886. At 16 Baldwin Street (*circled here*), events forced frightened and panicked residents to flee. The building no longer stands. *Sanborn Fire Insurance Map from Waterbury, New Haven County, Connecticut. Sanborn Map Company, Aug, 1890. Sheet 18. Map. https://www.loc.gov/item/sanborn01192_002/.*

day landmarks, it would have stood on a rise of property adjacent to the eastbound lanes of I-84, opposite Saint Mary's Hospital). Six families resided here during the spring of 1886 until frightening occurrences prompted them to evacuate the haunted house.

The bizarre happenings commenced sometime during the third week of May; up until that time, nothing out of the ordinary had been reported. Witnesses attributed the onset of these unexplainable events with the passing of John Shearon, the apartment house's popular landlord. For three years, neighbors were aware that Shearon suffered from a rheumatic condition; but they were startled when on May 6, 1886, he succumbed to bronchitis.[1] His age is variously listed as either fifty-three or fifty-five years old at the time of his death. Mary Shearon, John's wife, became the sole proprietor and continued to live in the house at 16 Baldwin Street.

In the days following John's funeral, residents began sharing stories about the peculiar noises they'd been hearing. The sounds, quiet and low at first, soon resembled a heavy barrel being rolled through the building. The inhabitants carefully searched for the source of the racket on each floor, from the basement to the upper rooms, but all in vain. During these May weeks, those hearing the ongoing tumult could not identify the cause of the noise or locate a possible reason for the disturbances. Within days of the banging sound's beginning, the situation grew worse.

Sisters Mary and Bridget Lawlor rented rooms on the first floor of 16 Baldwin Street. The house's supernatural entity seemed particularly focused on young Mary. Shortly after John Shearon's death, Mary was consumed by an overbearing feeling of sadness. Retreating to bed for days, her morose condition only worsened. During mid-May, while Mary Lawlor lay infirm, she became even more "oppressed with a strange feeling"[2] of sorrow. Upon looking up, she saw a "thick black cloud" materialize.[3] This undulating black shape moved along the ceiling. Mary explained that when the floating mass came in contact with the side wall, it disappeared into the structure "without apparent means of egress."[4] Witnessing the black shape floating through her room left Mary physically exhausted and severely ill.

Neighbors shared how Mary Shearon had observed the ghost of her husband roaming throughout the house as well. The widow suddenly felt as if there was someone watching her. Searching the room, she was surprised to discover the translucent shape of her husband under their bed. Taken aback by the vision, the landlady firmly commanded the specter, "Come out from under the bed, John!" Whereupon, in front of her incredulous eyes, John Shearon's ghostly form slowly dissolved and vanished.[5]

Whatever the source of the transparent entity might have been, it also took on a foreboding corporeal shape. Such was the experience of young Mary Lawlor, who was sent shrieking out from her first-floor rooms. Even after Mary's screaming pleas had summoned neighbors to her side, the insensate Miss Lawlor continued, unabated, to pound on her neighbors' doors despite the crowds' attempts to calm her. Slowly becoming aware of her safe surroundings, the frightened woman shared a disconcerting story. Inside her apartment at 16 Baldwin Street she'd seen a "strange figure of a human being." Whimpering, Mary paused to catch her breath before gasping, it was a man "with a wolf's head." The man-wolf stood before her, its arms swaying side to side, the monster's pointed ears were alert and its thick tongue salivating. The demon-beast suddenly lunged forward and grabbed Mary by her hair, "causing intense pain." Miss Lawlor wrestled free from the entity and madly ran for help.[6]

If anyone in the neighborhood doubted the events occurring inside widow Shearon's house, the unnerving Lawlor story proved something ungodly was indeed taking place. The supernatural experiences became too much for the families residing at 16 Baldwin Street. On Sunday, May 23, 1886, a renter by the name of Mrs. Gallivan became alarmed by the unexplained noises. Three days later, the Gallivan family packed their belongings and retreated to the Dennis Shea house across the street. Other tenants, like the Martin family, frightened by the stories about the apartment building in which they were living, also decided it was prudent to leave. They moved in with Bridget McGinn down the street at 69 Baldwin. The Lawlor sisters, too, had had enough, and on Thursday, May 27, they made plans to relocate. The neighborhood had already been inundated with rumors of the strange happenings occurring inside 16 Baldwin Street, so when they saw the Lawlors readying their furniture and other belongings in front of the apartment building for the movers, crowds began to gather. By evening, the sisters had departed; but the mob, milling about until ten o'clock that night, were still "waiting to see what [the Lawlors] did not want to see."

Of the six families renting rooms at 16 Baldwin Street, only three occupants remained: the seventy-nine-year-old widow Sophia Moore, too old to fear ghosts, steadfastly refused to flee (she'd resided in the house for eleven years); another tenant, a Mrs. Burger, stayed; and of course, the landlady, Mary Shearon, stood pat.[7]

Mary Shearon was at a loss for what to do. She felt that the damning stories were invented by Mary Lawlor, who, Shearon noted, was prone to hysterics. During the intervening days, conflicting rumors spread like wildfire. Some journalists had the widow Shearon experiencing nothing, while others gossiped that she was a direct witness to the bizarre events. Mary Shearon reasoned aloud to one newspaperman, "My husband was a quiet, harmless man who was dearly beloved by his neighbors and would not hurt a child."[8] Shearon then bowed her head and cried.

Finding lodgers to fill her apartment house became an exceedingly difficult chore. Stories about the noises and ghosts became common knowledge across the city. No one wanted to wake in the night to thunderous banging or see dark floating shapes, or bump into a half-human, wolf-headed monstrosity. Early in June 1886, a letter to the editor appeared in the *Waterbury Daily Republican*. The short missive, penned by another Baldwin Street resident, Julia Haynes, related how Daniel Vance O'Brien, a neighbor who lived at 32 Baldwin Street, "succeeded in capturing the ruffian who acted as ghost in the Shearon house." O'Brien, the letter intoned, gave the unnamed hoaxer a vicious thrashing and locked him in a room until the remaining residents of 16 Baldwin Street were able to look upon the culprit's visage. Oddly, the letter-writer never mentioned the perpetrator's identity. The offender would remain anonymous, the letter stated, "out of respect for [the faker's] friends who hold very respectful positions in [Waterbury] social circles."[9]

Was the letter an attempt to exorcize the horror stories associated with the demon house? No reason was given as to why the unidentified man wished to terrorize Mary Shearon or, for that matter, frighten anyone else in the home. Or, why acting as a ghost, he desired to harm the widow's reputation. Explanation was also lacking as to how the criminal entered the house, remained hidden in the home or created the assortment of strange noises and otherworldly visions. The epistle opened with the statement, "By publishing the following you will greatly favor Mrs. Shearon." Was this communication a ploy to absolve the house of its haunted character and thus influence prospective renters to consider lodging here? Perhaps only the wolf-headed humanoid creature knows for sure.

QUITTING TIME

The Waterbury factory was unnamed. But the following story did run in the *Times-Union* of Albany, New York, a well-respected newspaper. Here are the facts according to the March 4, 1901 article.[10]

Samuel Lukes had just returned to work. Several months back, he'd been severely hurt on the job. In fact, Samuel had lost an arm. Doctors weren't certain that the injured patient would survive. But Samuel Lukes was tough, and he did survive. And though life moved on for Sam, things were scarcely the same. Workers in those days of hard fact and harsher realities, had never even heard of health insurance, and factories—well, factory owners—pretty much couldn't care less about an injured laborer. There was always a new hire waiting outside the factory's fence eager to grab employment. But Lukes was in luck. Management took kindly to Sam's plight. They offered him a new position. Sure, it might be light duty, but the job did provide a regular paycheck, and how else could a man pay his way through life? Samuel Lukes was ecstatic. The prodigal one-armed man was wholeheartedly welcomed back to the factory by his overjoyed friends.

It was now February, several blissful weeks since Samuel Lukes had returned to work, when unexpectedly the injury took a turn for the worse. Lukes was once again hospitalized. Was it blood poisoning? A lingering infection? No one could tell why the patient continually weakened. Tragically, the all too brief reprieve Samuel Lukes had received from Heaven expired. The hospital's doctors sadly shook their heads as the factory worker took his final breath and died.

Ironically, it wasn't long after poor Samuel's death that spring seemingly arrived early and filled Waterbury's late-winter world with energizing warmth and hope. During one of these refreshing spring-like evenings, a supernatural event took place. The factory was closed and deserted, except for "the watchman and his assistants," when one of the guards found the dedicated Lukes standing in front of his machine. "Sam," the watchman announced, "it's after 6 o'clock; why don't you go home?"

"All right," replied the grinning one-armed man. Sam looked over toward the beckoning and unseasonably pleasant February-filled windows. "I am going away in a few minutes."[11]

The watchman bid Sam goodnight and turned away. He was several steps distant from the mill-hand when suddenly it dawned on the guard: Samuel Lukes was dead. Good God, he'd died weeks ago. The watchman screamed in terror and fled through the factory. He tripped and fell badly, dislocating his shoulder. Calling for help, the other watchmen on duty responded. After being helped to his feet, the shocked guard shared the animated story of his talking with a dead man. His colleagues shook their heads and guffawed in the guard's anxious face. Unwaveringly, over the ensuing days, the guard repeated his frightening experience of meeting the ghost of Samuel Lukes. At first, the incredulous factory workers all laughed at the unbelievable story. But soon enough, after considering what transpired, they weren't laughing so readily.[12] During the intervening months, as warmer weather grew closer, there remained a pervasive darkness that seemed to hold on to the workroom where the dead man had been seen. This pall was felt by all the workers. All the mill hands except for smiling Samuel Lukes, who, finally, had left the building.

EVICTED BY A GHOST

Discovering that one's home might be haunted would clearly generate a spectrum of terrifying emotions. Imagine, at any moment, some inexplicable event could occur: frightening visions, unearthly sounds, objects levitating on their own, cold spots—the array of shuddering possibilities is mind-wracking. It's a wonder that folks can calmly remain ensconced inside the four walls of what, in reality, has become a supernatural prison. Now, consider for a moment, the magnified horrors that would confront terrified tenants whose living quarters are possessed by a demented paranormal proprietor?

Such is the jarring experience of several shocked Waterbury families who found themselves out-of-doors when they fell victim to their lurid landlord's eldritch evictions. Or worse yet, not just unceremoniously booted to the curb but actually woken from unconsciousness to find that they were propped atop the roof of their own house. Such a vengeful wraith-landlord actually did control property in downtown Waterbury. According to the Jazz Age ghost researcher Oliver E. Carruth, such a situation existed in a tall two-and-a-half-story house, once located on South Willow Street.

The story goes that sometime during the latter half of the nineteenth century, a gentleman moved into this Waterbury home known for its sharply slanting roof. On the occasion of the very first late-night storm, the new owner was startled awake by a number of strange noises emanating throughout house. These sounds came to an abrupt halt with an unearthly "sobbing wail."[13] Determined to locate the source of the fearsome racket, the man tried to leave his bed but was thrown back and restrained on the mattress by an invisible force. This was the last thing the fellow remembered until the following rainy morning. A passerby pointed out the tenant's supine figure, still adorned in nightclothes, stretched across the slanting roof of the tall house. It's important to note that "there was no trap door [leading to] the roof and no way of reaching it except by ladder."[14]

Neighbors scampered to the roof with a borrowed ladder and carried the unconscious man from his bizarre perch. It took some time to revive him. He had no memory of how he arrived on the roof. Rapt, his liberators leaned toward the stunned fellow, who could only vaguely relate the circumstances of the previous evening's odd and noisy events leading up to his rooftop rescue. More frighteningly, each time the man spent a rainy night in his home, the dramatic rooftop rescues needed repeating. His Waterbury tenancy did not last long.

Scoffing at the ridiculously weird tales circulating around South Willow Street, another family decided that the low rent was too good an offer to ignore. Embracing their luck, the new tenants guffawed at their neighbors' unfounded fears. "Pshaw," quipped the incredulous newest owners when confronted by the wild ghost stories. And they remained in the house, refusing to believe in the supernatural.

Until it rained.

One evening, not too long afterward, knowledgeable neighbors began to look askance at the ominous clouds gathering overhead. Once it was dark, they realized, this would be the new family's initiation to an overnight rainfall. Sure enough, the following morning, the home's male adult occupant was found reclined on the roof in a pronounced stupor. Vigorously shaken awake, he groggily focused on his rescuers standing on the top rungs of a ladder leaning nearby. The fellow was completely unaware as to how he came to spend the entire night on the shingles of his slanted roof. The latest victims of this bizarre rooftop banishment packed their belongings and fled. After this family moved away, the house remained abandoned for a long period of time.

Anxious to discern any possible reason that might lead to an explanation of these squall-induced roof evictions, local residents delved into the neighborhood's history. "Investigators who suspected that a ghost had put the men on the roof dug up the story of a peddler who had asked for lodging at the house on a stormy night."[15] Supposedly, the story went, this peddler proceeded out to the barn behind the house to check on his horse just as it started to rain. "The next morning, he was found dead under his wagon, slain by robbers who believed his goods were valuable."[16] The haunted home's roof-sleuths surmised that on stormy nights, this peddler's ghost was determined to place male tenants of the abode out of the reach of any thieves or murderers and set them safely on top of the house. Others were inclined to think that the peddler's spirit was determined to drag others from their sleep because he himself was "deprived of a bed on the same kind of [tempestuous] night."[17]

The actual source of this peculiar haunting might date to the 1870s. A markedly similar tale states that during January 1871, a Waterbury family, on acquiring a new residence, proceeded to move their furniture into the home. When the deliverymen returned the following morning to deliver the remainder of the couple's belongings, the movers were ordered to repack everything and return it to this family's previous address. Perplexed by the abrupt turnabout in plans, the movers were informed by the homeowners that they refused to live in a haunted house. Over the course of their first night in the home, the wife had been regaled by neighbors' stories concerning the strange activity centering on the place. Wide-eyed, she heard about the house experiencing an inordinate number of deaths. In addition, it was shared that a former owner "found himself and his wife, about 2 o'clock one morning, standing in the middle of the street in their night robes. They had no idea as to how they came [to be standing] there."[18] The paranormal litany was more than the new owner could bear. Following that family's departure in 1871, the house assumed an ominous reputation. It remained abandoned for years. Whatever the reason, the ghostly landlord obviously preferred solitude during dark and stormy nights.

DISTURBER OF GRAVES: WHEN THE CITY HALL SPECTER CALLS

"Grave! Grave! thou art not my home."
—Nathaniel Hawthorne, "Graves and Goblins," 1835

In April 1922, fervent Spiritualist Arthur Conan Doyle, the world-famous creator of Sherlock Holmes, captivated wide-eyed audiences at Carnegie Hall with his lectures concerning psychic phenomena.[19] While the mystery writer was enthralling New York City with his observations about ghostly manifestations, the paranormal stage was simultaneously set in the Naugatuck Valley for a unique brand of spiritual theater. A specter adorned in colonial military garb was seen strutting down the halls of Waterbury's city hall.

The whispers had begun during April, the cruelest of months (T.S. Eliot's poem *The Waste Land* would be published by year's end). On Friday, April 14, 1922, Timothy Horgan, superintendent of the municipal building, came forward to publicly announce that he'd seen the figure of a shadow man wearing the uniform of a Continental soldier.[20] It was night, Horgan related, and he was handling his rounds, only to be surprised upon discovering someone still in the building. Perhaps, thought Horgan,

Hallowed and Haunted Halls. Following the previous city hall's destruction by arson, Waterbury's new municipal building (constructed 1914–15) became the residence of a colonial ghost. *Author's collection.*

the fellow was a job seeker who somehow got himself locked inside after hours. But before the civil servant could confront the strange visitor, the supernatural intruder turned and quickly paced down the hall toward the doors of the connected firehouse and vanished. After the building superintendent admitted that he had witnessed something unearthly, other denizens of city hall stepped out from their self-imposed silence concerning their own personal paranormal experiences. This bevy of administrative heavy-hitters included Police Chief George M. Beach, Judge John F. McGrath and Prosecuting Attorney James A. Peasley. Each man reluctantly explained that they too had come in contact with a similar ghostly image just a day earlier, on Thursday, April 13.

In this particular supernatural instance, the traditional stormy-night inspiration for summoning spirits was not required; it was nine o'clock in the morning when Police Chief Beach saw the ghost wandering along the second-floor corridor. He watched disbelievingly as the specter continued down the hallway and passed into the courtroom; here, Judge McGrath would later admit, he caught sight of the spirit in his peripheral vision before it passed into the lawyers' chambers. At this point, Attorney Peasley witnessed the phantom. All concurred that the shape they saw was that of a male Revolutionary War soldier.[21]

The even-keeled jurists sought a rational explanation for the mysterious wanderer. Immediately, these stalwart witnesses set out to locate the city printer, Peter Shea, who happened to be a member of the Mattatuck Drum Corps. They figured, logically, that in preparation for some official affair, Shea could have arrived at work wearing his regimental costume. But printer Pete explained that he'd been in his shop, hard at work, all morning. In fact, Pete stressed that even if he had desired to wear his uniform on the day the ghost was seen, it would have been impossible; his formal military outfit was at that very moment being pressed for an upcoming parade.

To some city workers, the apparition's arrival came as no surprise. The night watchman, John Clunny, and the tax collector, Jesse Devine, frequently heard unexplained noises while they were in the building alone.[22] Following confirmation that additional eyewitnesses had come in contact with a supernatural image, Devine set out each night in search of the eldritch visitant.

Within a few days, the taxman turned ghost hunter was certain that he'd capture an honest-to-goodness spook when the court stenographers ran shrieking past his office doorway. Responding to these terrified shouts, the breathless clerks shared with Devine how they'd watched a strange "white-shaped thing" glide down the main staircase, turn a corner and head determinedly into the basement. Jesse Devine, along with City Clerk Kelly, who'd both been dedicated to tracking the ghost, raced into the lower-level laboratory. However, they were promptly disappointed by what they uncovered: the entity proved to be a most terrestrial flesh-and-blood creature. The man in white turned out to be none other than the city's bacteriologist, John Lyon; he was dressed in his protective lab gear.[23]

Was the entire monthlong haunting an elaborate hoax? One question to ask is, why would civic leaders expose themselves to ridicule over seeing a ghost? In this regard, Police Chief George Beach was a no-nonsense professional who was viewed as a "strict disciplinarian [who always] required his men [to] rigidly adhere to departmental rules and order."[24] Beach was not an administrative head prone to jocularity, and though reluctant to admit it publicly, Chief Beach gave a positive nod to having seen something when queried afterward. In addition, a reporter with the *Waterbury Republican* wrote that those "who are supposed to have seen it [the ghost] will not admit so outright, [though] they make strange intimations that looks as tho [*sic*] they must have seen something."[25]

Most people around the Brass City took for granted that something eerie would eventually happen in or around city hall. This was because of the building's proximity to the old Grand Street Cemetery that once loomed next door. Waterbury's new city hall (built in 1915) was seven years old when the paranormal disturbances began. Civil servants, indeed all of Waterbury's citizens, were aware that the building was constructed not merely next to but possibly on top of a portion of the ancient burial ground. The April 15, 1922 *Waterbury Republican* wrote, "A number of Revolutionary soldiers were buried [in the Grand Street Cemetery] and the workmen who have recently been remodeling the park dug into the bones of several of them" (in 1922, plans were enacted to alter the park's driveways).[26] Was the city hall ghost vengeful about his being woken from an eternal slumber? Not so tongue-in-cheek, a Waterbury newspaper opined, "It is assumed that this action [of unceremoniously uncovering human remains] so disturbed the ghost of one of [the soldiers] that he started for [city hall] to put in a complaint the same as all good citizens."[27]

The Last Library on the Left or, How Far the Mighty Fallen Fell

Any mention of a possible city hall ghost needs to be placed in context. And all skeletal fingers point to the story of the abandoned burial grounds next door. The old Grand Street Cemetery (where the Silas Bronson Library now stands) was situated on a hillock that once overlooked the Naugatuck River. The cemetery was bound approximately by Grand and Meadow Streets and the now-vanished Hall Street. The consecrated land embraced Waterbury's dead dating back to 1709 (although mention exists of the locality being dubbed "Burying-Yard Hill" as early as 1695). Use of the Grand Street Cemetery began tapering off in 1853 due to the opening of the Riverside Cemetery across town (beside the Naugatuck River). Once the relocation of

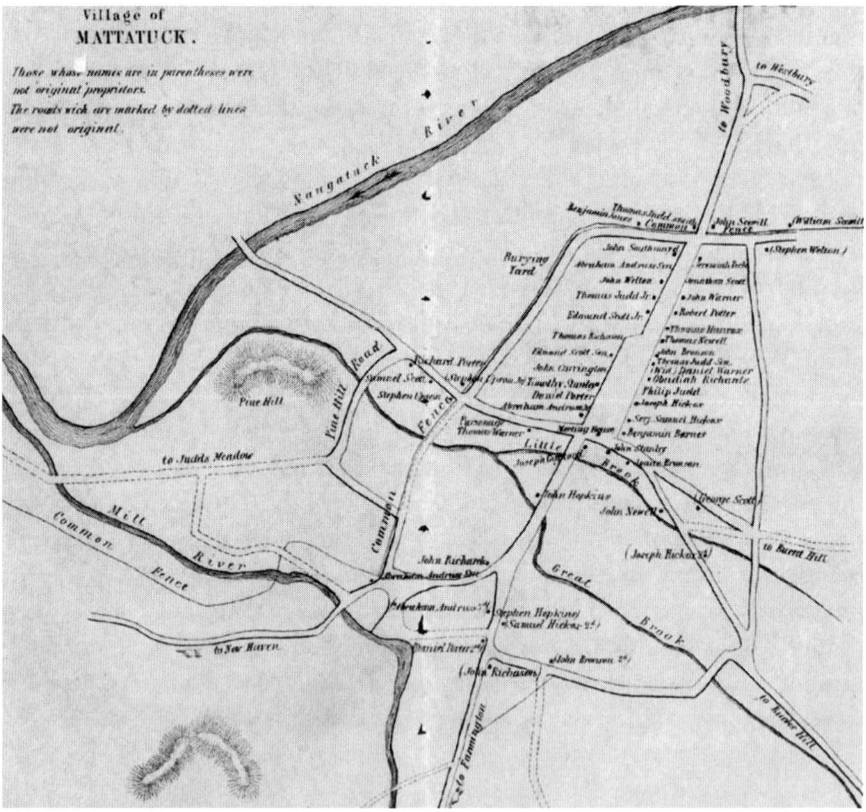

Which Way to the Cemetery? Waterbury's first burial grounds were situated beyond the bustling living area of the city's earliest settlement as seen on this 1680s map of Mattatuck Village. *From Henry Bronson,* The History of Waterbury, Connecticut, *Bronson Brothers, 1858.*

Abandoned Cemetery in the Midst of Downtown. Known as the Grand Street Cemetery, these grounds ceased being utilized around 1850. Over the intervening years, the cemetery became derelict and, perhaps worse, desecrated. *Grand Street Cemetery, Photograph Collection, CT-02, Max R. Traurig Library. Mattatuck Museum. Waterbury, CT.*

Grand Street Cemetery's inhabitants by family members had commenced, "from the old to the new [Riverside Cemetery] for reburial the old place soon showed the effect....Re-opened graves, with fragments of coffins left uncovered...overturned headstones and footstones became features of the place, and before many years had passed, the ground was overgrown with weeds, briers and bushes."[28]

By the end of the nineteenth century, the Grand Street Cemetery's physical appearance had become a spirited bone of contention between factions wanting to repurpose the land for a public park and library and those who wished to preserve the sacred graves of Waterbury's founders. The one item all parties agreed on was the horrid condition that had befallen the now-closed burial grounds. Blighted with open graves and scattered coffins, the boneyard had taken on a forlorn and ghastly presence in the midst of downtown. The rector of St. Patrick's Church, Reverend John H. Duggan, lamented, "I am pained every time I pass on Meadow Street and see bones exposed in the cemetery."[29] Adding to this deplorable state, an unattractive tall wooden fence enclosed large sections of the cemetery,[30] which created a screen for illegal and illicit activity. The once proud graveyard disintegrated into a lamented eyesore, and "the place became a hangout for derelicts and a favorite spot for spooners [a popular early twentieth-century term for couples' carnal relations].[31]

Steps to address the old cemetery's decrepit condition began in 1882 when the Connecticut General Assembly voted to allow the land of the old Waterbury cemetery to be appropriated for use as a park or civic building. Following eight years of outcry, on May 1, 1890, Mayor Charles R. Baldwin arranged a public meeting where all interested parties could voice an opinion. Turns out, the courtroom was not large enough to accommodate the boisterous crowd. Heated arguments arose with speakers on either side of the issue thundering that the Grand Street Cemetery was an "abomination," accompanied by demands to remove all the remaining bodies, while other speakers "very vigorously" bellowed that anyone "who would remove the body of a relative was a savage!"[32] That night, a resolution was unanimously passed by the board of aldermen for the city to appropriate the old cemetery land for public usage.

Less than a year later, on Friday April 24, 1891, a large crew of men began removing the pitted and leaning headstones that lay scattered across the overgrown cemetery's now-deconsecrated grounds. The following day's *New Haven Register* lamented on page 1, "Workmen have begun to obliterate the oldest cemetery in [Waterbury]."[33] Waterbury preservationist Sarah J. Prichard dubbed this "Waterbury's 'Black Friday'" and poetically intoned, "No longer can the moon look down" on the gravestones of the city's noble, but shunned, ancestors.[34] Sadly, it was announced that the graves to which no living descendent could be contacted would result in those "remains [being] left untouched and the headstones [buried]."[35] This disturbing decision meant that the headstones were "sunken out of sight [in the earth]—sometimes, but not always, over the graves to which they belonged. In some cases, two or three stones were buried together. The remainder [of headstones] were placed in what was once [known as] 'the vault.'"[36]

Three days later, on April 27, 1891, the largescale removal of remains commenced.[37] The sorrowful business of "taking up the bodies in the Grand Street Cemetery for interment elsewhere" struck a sour chord with many citizens. Sturges Judd (the cemetery's custodian from 1862 until 1891) noted in a grief-stricken tone, "The sensation of opening a grave to remove the remains of a friend, to find nothing but a few rusty screws or nails, or possibly, a few scattered bones, is something the majority of people care to experience but once."[38]

The untenably morbid situation created by still-buried bodies and hidden gravestones was exacerbated later that same summer. In July 1891, the city's library representatives voted to accept the new park (and former cemetery grounds) as the location to build the Silas Bronson Library. Construction on the library started in June 1893 with predictably somber results: when the building's foundation was excavated, a plethora of graves were rediscovered. Tossing these stone epitaphs off to the side, the laborers continued with the construction project. Neglected and underfoot, the tablets were trod on and, worse yet, crushed under the weight of draft horses that were pulling heavy carts. Realizing, much too late, just how many headstones had been pulverized beyond repair, the workers stacked the surviving stones in the now completed library's basement. And there they lingered in darkness, waiting over four decades before being delivered once more into Waterbury historian Prichard's poetic moonlight. In 1934, the grave markers that had been stored in the library's basement were elegantly framed within Library Park's brick retaining wall along Meadow Street.

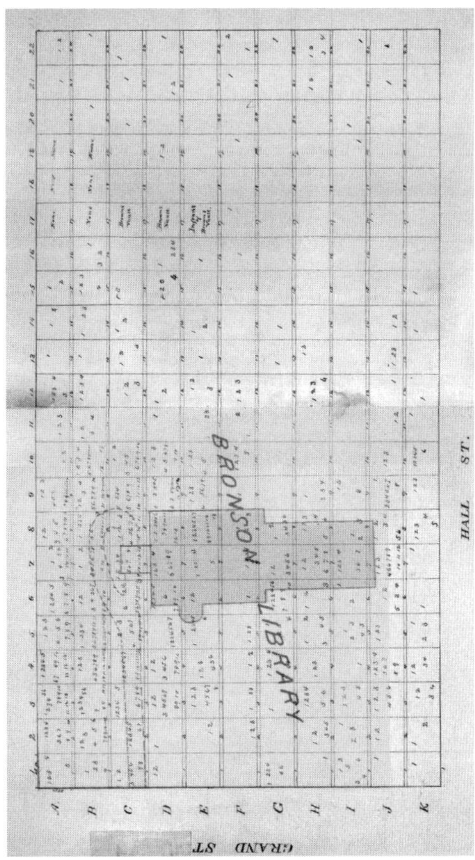

Sacred and Shared Ground. This burial chart, painstakingly created by Sturges Judd (Grand Street Cemetery's caretaker from 1862 to 1891), illustrates where the original Silas Bronson Library stood. Approximately three thousand graves were located adjacent to, as well as beneath, the library. How many bodies might yet remain in Library Park? *Grand Street Cemetery Map Overlay, Fortune Research Collection, M-43, Max R. Traurig Library. Mattatuck Museum. Waterbury, CT.*

Don't Look in the Basement. Upon completion of the first Silas Bronson Library in 1893, construction workers gathered the cemetery's unclaimed headstones and placed them in the building's cellar. The chiseled death's heads remained here, hidden from view for more than a generation. *Author's collection.*

New Life for Old Gravestones. Since 1934, the retaining wall for Library Park (situated along Meadow Street) has hosted the abandoned grave markers that were once stored in the cellar of the Bronson Library. *Photograph by Michael J. Bielawa, taken April 27, 2024.*

And what of the possibility of another vengeful ghost resurfacing inside city hall? Or, for that matter, could a spirit commence pacing the stacks of the newer, beautiful Bronson Library? These are the questions that might be answered when the next shovel plunges into Library Park's storied earth.

BOUND WITH A DREAM: THE SECOND LIFE OF LULU MORDEN

Dream is a second life.
—*Gérard de Nerval,* Aurélia

I thought to find Love in the heat of day…
But sweet Love is the comforter of night.
—*William Blake*

I could sleep, I could sleep
When I lived alone
Is there a ghost in my house?
—*From the song "Is There a Ghost" by Band of Horses*

Lulu Morden blushed with anticipation just knowing how soon she'd again be in the arms of her true love. And there he was, suddenly standing before her: tall, handsome, smiling.

Born in Nebraska in 1866, the young firebrand Lucena Mandana Morden realized from an early age that she was in conflict with the world around her. Wrestling with the staid and constricting norms of the Victorian era, she saucily announced to her high school classmates in Concordia, Kansas: "Call me Lulu!" Coming of age and seeking gainful employment, Lulu discovered that conventionality would never suit her. Sure, she'd become a midwestern teacher, and afterward, living in the Pacific Northwest, Lulu reluctantly pounded away on the steel pads of a Bartholomew stenograph machine. But all the while, Lulu had bigger designs in mind, and the avant-garde woman set her sights on becoming an inventor.

Lulu longingly stretched onto her tiptoes, pressing her pulsating heart tightly against the muscular chest of the beautiful man she adored.

Since her days attending Teachers' College in Emporia, Kansas, Lulu had been fascinated with mechanical engineering, and in 1900, she was awarded her first patent: a type of ring-bound notebook. Lulu understood society's game, and she signed her patent application with the masculine moniker L.M. Morden. She'd continue devising and perfecting a variety of designs for notebook-binders and loose-leaf books. Eventually, L.M. Morden would be granted an impressive total of forty-seven patents. Moving her business stratagems forward, Lulu sought a modern industrial setting where she could fabricate her blueprint visions, which brought her to the shores of the Naugatuck River.

The Indomitable Lucena Mandana Morden. Pictured with her high school class in 1884 (*middle of back row*), the dynamic Kanas teenager preferred to be addressed as Lulu. Later in life, she supposedly became possessed by a Dream-Spirit-Lover. *Photo from* Prairie Portrait: Centennial Book Concordia 1871–1971. *Courtesy of Concordia Junior-Senior High School, Concordia, KS.*

Waterbury proved the perfect site, and after relocating her factory to larger and better outfitted buildings across the city, her Morden Manufacturing Corporation was firmly established inside the sixteen rooms of the former E.T. Turner mansion.[39] The sprawling place, located on the corner of Johnson Street and Chestnut Avenue, simultaneously served as both Lulu's factory and home. And to the surprise of many, it also proved to be Lulu's love nest.

Lulu threw her arms around the neck of her one true love…

By the mid-1920s, folks living all along the Naugatuck Valley viewed Morden's life as a glittering fairy-tale success. Lulu's ingenious ring-binders had symbolically bound together a mansion, a bustling factory and wealth—it was reported that the single lady was worth a cool half million dollars. And her prolific vision was a boon to the local economy: Morden Manufacturing employed three hundred workers. But it was her mysterious lover who filled Lulu's heart and fueled Waterbury gossip. It seemed odd, but no one (and there were many sets of prying eyes) had ever witnessed anyone, let alone a tall, handsome man, entering the palatial front doors of the Morden home.

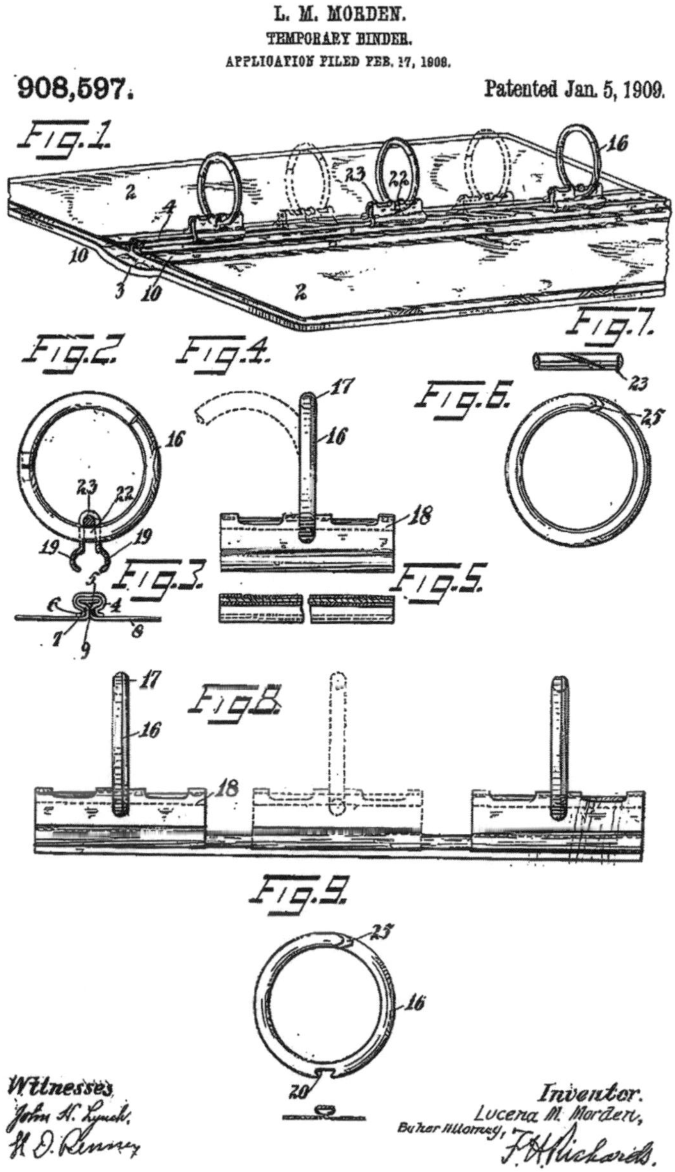

Waterbury's prolific inventor Lulu Morden patented this notebook binder in 1909. Lulu's creative genius led her to being credited with a total of forty-seven patents. Items were manufactured in her Waterbury factory-home on Johnson Street. *Morden, Lucena M. Temporary Binder. US Patent 0908597, filed February 7, 1908, and issued January 5, 1909.*

In fact, if it wasn't for Lulu's relating her passionate tales of wooing and love-making—to say nothing of the astute business advice provided by her beloved mystery-gentleman—her neighbors wouldn't have believed in the existence of such a deep-seated romance.

The embracing couples' frenzied lips met as Lulu's body shuddered within her man's clasp—and then she bolted upright in bed. Upright and wide awake. And very, very, alone in her huge, deserted Waterbury mansion.

Sometime around 1926, it appears that the rich factory owner began sharing a remarkable and sordid story with Waterbury residents. Certainly, Lulu expressed, she had scads of money and material things. But Lulu confided that her devotion to the business world had denied her any friends.[40] Lulu admitted that her "brooding loneliness" was devastating. And then one day, as if in response to a prayer (was it a prayer answered by heaven or hell?), a lover arrived in Lulu's life. Lulu explained to her curious, and then concerned, neighbors, that her romantic gentleman was a "phantom" who existed only in the realm of her sleeping world. Morden declared that "each

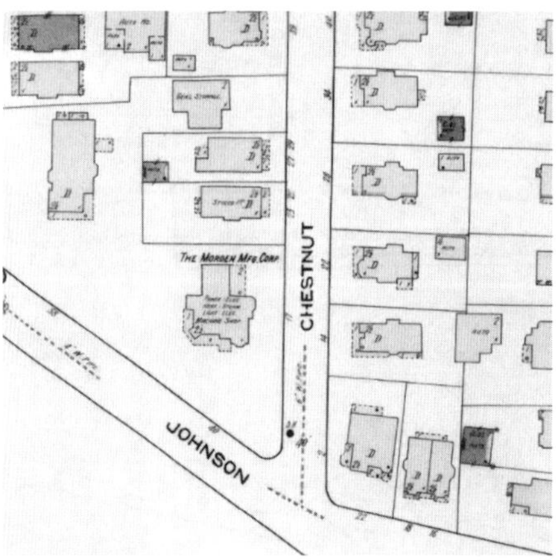

Left: (Bad) Dream House. When Lulu Morden acquired this property, she converted a portion of the house into a manufactory. Reportedly, her dream-spirit-lover was a frequent visitor here. *Sanborn Fire Insurance Map from Waterbury, New Hven County, Connecticut. Sanborn Map Company; Vol. 1, 1922. Sheet 35. Map. https://www.loc.gov/item/sanborn01192_005/.*

Right: Waterbury Home of the Dream-Spirit-Lover. Perhaps the only existing illustration of Lulu Morden's home and factory as it appeared during her lifetime. The wealthy inventor shared how she was often advised by a dream-entity in this house. *T.M. Fowler and Hughes & Bailey. Aero view of Waterbury, Connecticut. Boston, Hughes & Fowler, 1917. Map. https://www.loc.gov/item/gm71005376/.*

night in her dreams she and the man she worshipped lived a life of high adventure." Lulu continued to relate that she and her man "talked to each other and journeyed hand-in-hand through the land of dreams."[41] Lulu proudly stated that this nighttime phantom made love to her and advised her regarding business affairs.[42]

Writing about Lulu, the *New York American* on December 23, 1926, noted that her experience resembled a contemporary surreal novel titled *The Cream of the Jest*. In this fictional work, author James Branch Cabell wrote of "nightly adventures with an imagined sweetheart whose beauty surpasses the loveliness" of all mortals.

But of late, Lulu was at a terrible loss. The alarmed factory owner admitted that she'd been abandoned by her phantom lover. Suddenly, he no longer arrived at her nocturnal bedside to escort her into the only ecstasy she'd ever known: the second life that existed in her romantic dream-dimension had dissolved. Lost within a morose daze, Lulu took to sleeplessly wandering her vast and lonely mansion in search of her lost lover. "Where did my man vanish off to?," she pondered. "Yes, I am successful, yes I am wealthy, but I am lonely." Oh, so terribly lonely.

Word about Lulu losing her phantom lover ran rampant throughout Waterbury in late December 1926.[43] A neighbor of the secluded factory owner reasoned, "When her dream wooer vanished…Lulu considered life unlivable."[44] Absent her rapt and adoring phantom-dream-lover, Lulu chose a dire path.

It was four days before Christmas 1926 when Lulu Morden, inside her Johnson Street home, gathered all the bedclothes she could find. Meticulously, the "jilted" lover tacked quilts over the windows and wedged sheets into the kitchen's doorframes. The inventor examined her last desperate handiwork. Just before sitting down in a chair she purposely placed in the center of the kitchen, the dejected woman turned six dials of her gas oven to the on position. Sorely weighed down by the sadness engulfing her lonely existence, Lulu leaned back and inhaled the deadly fumes.

The Morden mansion's longtime custodian and gardener, Frederick M. Feest, arrived at Lulu's house as he usually did on Monday morning and twice more that same day (December 20, 1926) in order to fire the furnace. But finding the doors locked and with no one responding to the bell, he figured that Morden had perchance stepped out due to last-minute Christmas plans. On the following morning, finding the house dark once again, Feest surmised that something was most certainly amiss.[45] Summoning the police, they together entered the mansion. A pungent stench of gas filled the building while the officers and Feest, with handkerchiefs pressed to their faces, raced from room to room calling out for Morden. They found Lulu dead, reposed in the chair she had set in the middle of her kitchen. Paperwork was neatly arranged on the floor around her. A letter Lulu had prepared expressed that her final actions were of her own volition. There were additional documents addressed to the Waterbury National Bank concerning her ultimate financial decisions. There was no mention of her dream lover. She was sixty years old.

LUCENA MANDANA MORDEN, THE midwestern teacher-spinster turned New England inventor and rich factory owner, had found herself in the Brass City living a tarnished dream. After her funeral, Lulu's bankers and attorney closed the large doors of her mansion one last time as they collectively shook a bowed head—such a sad loss, such a shame. But now, as the mansion's doors locked shut this final time, just perhaps…just maybe…

Lulu Morden again blushed with anticipation—she would soon be in the arms of her true love, suddenly standing before her in their ethereal paradise.[46]

2
House of Thorn and Echo
Rose Hill Cottage

Part One: It Is Born Bad

Rose Hill Cottage was born bad. Well, that's what Alexander Dallas, the gardener, thought. And that burly, bearded, redheaded titan should know. Over the decades, Alexander had sown the ground as master landscaper for one of Waterbury's richest and most privileged owners of the massive mansion known as Rose Hill. The gardener had his hands in the dirt surrounding that palace for so many years, folks said he himself had taken root on the hill. It was back in those days, turning the soil atop Prospect Hill, that Alexander became privy to all sorts of strange happenings at the Rose Hill manor. Thus follows the gardener's observations.[1]

Prospect Hill became the sought-after destination for Waterbury's elite beginning with William Henry Scovill, the wealthiest man in town. Scovill constructed one of the first houses on the hill as a dandy wedding present for his daughter. After her marriage in 1851, her house would overlook what became the city's grand center green. It was around this same time that William and his brother James consolidated some of the city's brass factories into the vast Scovill Manufacturing empire.

Alexander Dallas never knew William Scovill; he had died well before the gardener's services were provided at Rose Hill. The redheaded Scotsman regularly looked at a portrait of the old man that a Parisian artist had rendered posthumously of the industrialist. The man had a

Left: Waterbury Industrialist William Henry Scovill (1796–1854). Scovill was the original owner of Rose Hill Cottage. Not long after moving into the mansion, both William and his wife, Rebecca, confronted madness and death. *Illustration from, Joseph Anderson, editor.* The Town and City of Waterbury, Connecticut, From the Aboriginal Period to the Year Eighteen Hundred and Ninety-Five, *The Price & Lee Company, 1896. pdf. https://www.loc.gov/item/98000206/.*

Below: Rose Hill Cottage Today. A lot of changes have taken place during the nearly two centuries since the mansion was born, both to the house's elaborate appearance and the surrounding neighborhood. The one constant are the ghosts roaming the house and its grounds. *Photograph by Michael J. Bielawa, taken May 27, 2022.*

large forehead, full sideburns and a squat white rectangle of a beard low on his chin.

In 1852, Scovill engaged the famous New Haven architect Henry Austin to build a stately residence in the Gothic Cottage style. The home would be regarded as the "finest and costliest place in town."[2] His big house was set near the middle part of this rising hill across from his daughter's gifted mansion. Scovill was certainly proud of his own place. The innards of the house were adorned with a medieval flower design. The rose motif appeared throughout the Scovill mansion. Roses and vines had been carved on the molding along the ceiling, roses were etched in the stained-glass windows, wooden roses bloomed on the main hall's banister, mosaic roses grew underfoot in the floor's tile design. Those roses were how the mansion got its name.

The house was hardly completed when Mrs. Rebecca Scovill, William's second wife, began acting weirdly. Word circulated that she became jakey from drink.[3] Others said Mrs. Scovill had turned raving mad. Old man Scovill could not take the stress of his wife's wild and emotional carryings-

A rose motif appears throughout the mansion's interior as seen here on the home's stained-glass windows. Roses are carved in the main hall's banister and fireplaces and set in the floor's tile work. This beautiful design led the home's first owner, William Scovill, to proudly christen the property Rose Hill Cottage. *Courtesy of the Greater Waterbury YMCA. Photograph by Michael J. Bielawa.*

Abandoned Rose Hill Cottage in 1856. The home was built for William and Rebecca Scovill during 1852–53, but the husband and wife tragically died soon after moving into the mansion, seemingly establishing a tradition of strange occurrences. *Rose Hill, Photograph Collection, CT-02, Max R. Traurig Library. Mattatuck Museum. Waterbury, CT.*

on. Suddenly, William got sick too. He began aging fast. William Scovill fled Rose Hill after nearly thirty years of marriage and went south, back to his hometown and friends in Charleston. But even far away from Rose Hill Cottage, Scovill continued to waste away. It was just a matter of time before the aged man became ancient. He died in South Carolina in March 1854. A few months after his death, Mrs. Scovill, back in Waterbury, passed away too—all alone and crazed, a prisoner trapped within the carved thorns of Rose Hill Cottage.

For a decade, the mansion and its cursed name lay abandoned. Over time, the place took on a frightening aspect. Folks passing by eyed the long meandering path leading to the forlorn manor and shuddered when reminded of the Scovills' eerie fate. These spectators had no idea just how terrible, and sad, a story would occupy this house of thorns.

Part Two: When Oranges Are Poisoned, Woe to Pick the Fruits of Rose Hill Cottage

Long after William and Rebecca Scovill died, a new family finally did move into the big house. Joseph Chauncey Welton, president of the Waterbury Brass Company and the Oakville Pin factory, purchased the place in 1863.[4] Welton was so rich that before living in Rose Hill, he and his kin resided nearby in a gaggle of rooms at the Brown Hotel. That hotel had been known as the Arcade because of the fine tall columns out front; it was located at the Exchange Place crossroads. When Welton finally dusted off some of that brass money, he bought the Cottage and hired gardener Alexander Dallas.

Beautiful Caroline Josephine Welton (1842–1884) was the daughter of wealthy brass baron Joseph Chauncey Welton. Recognized for her love of nature and talent as an equestrian, she was equally known for her eccentric mannerisms. After a mountain climbing tragedy, her ghost was reportedly witnessed in both Colorado and Connecticut. *Abraham Archibald Anderson (American, 1846–1940) Miss Caroline Welton, unknown date, oil on canvas, gift of The Society for Prevention of Cruelty to Animals, 1940; X68.3; Mattatuck Museum, Waterbury, CT.*

Welton was a strict authoritarian with no time for anything but business.[5] Come mornings, old man Welton would wake up and head directly for the front door of Rose Hill Cottage. Standing there on the front steps of the mansion in the day's early mist, he surveyed his brass empire. Welton made sure smoke was pouring out from the smokestacks—that way he knew the workers were in the factories and all was right with the world. Well, at least it was right with the world of the mill owners.[6]

As stern as the mill master might be, his wife, Jane, was the exact opposite: she was gregarious and cheerful. She loved to entertain with grand fetes for all of Waterbury's most sophisticated citizens. It was all the rage to be included on Mrs.

Welton's invitation list. Rose Hill Cottage was the place to be and the place to be seen. Fancy carriages lined Prospect Street all the way down to and around the Green for those gilded gatherings.

They had a daughter, Caroline Josephine Welton. Everyone called her Carrie. She had just turned twenty-one when the family moved into Rose Hill Cottage. Quite the slender dark beauty, mistress Carrie was the embodiment of a free spirit: strong-willed, demanding and, some might say, spoiled.[7] Her parents certainly loved her, but each Welton residing inside Rose Hill Cottage lived in a world of their own choosing. Her father was strictly business, while her mother tried to raise Carrie as the royal belle of Waterbury. The girl would have none of it. She was an independent lass, to say the least. She was cultured at all the best schools, and her mother introduced Carrie to the richest and most handsome young bachelors Connecticut could conjure. With a sniff, she turned her back on high society. Freedom and nature were what she sought. It was animals above all that she adored. But it was Carrie's absolute devotion to four-legged creatures that would soon enough destroy her whole family.

Carrie had a stallion, black as midnight. Knight of the Forest was his name; Carrie called him Knight. Her father acquired that horse as a gift for his daughter in 1865.[8] She took after her father in that one regard: they both loved horses and riding. The old man boarded several prize steeds on his property, but Carrie had a peculiar temperament when it came to Knight. Carrie's love for Knight was boundless. She had silver shoes, real sterling, mind you, made for the animal, and his stall was draped in velvet. Carrie fed that horse his oats from a special-crafted bone china bowl and plate that were hand-painted with pansies and the horse's name, Knight, in ornate gold letters.[9] Carrie Welton was certainly unique—uniquely eccentric. She'd ride Knight all over Waterbury, in all kinds of weather, be it rain, summer heat or snow. The strangest fact, however, definitely had to do with

Strong-willed Carrie Welton was known for her eccentricities. Wherever she went in public, Carrie was often seen wearing a pink domino mask like the one pictured here. *Drawing by Mary Iorio (1963–current),* Domino Mask, *Pen and Ink, 2025.*

her fashion choices. Whenever she ventured outside, Carrie was forever wearing a pink domino mask over her face. This is the sort of mask one usually sees worn at a fancy Carnival ball in Venice. Carrie never went anywhere without that mask!

One night, after attending to business in New York City, Mr. Welton returned to Waterbury aboard the seven o'clock train. He had just entered Rose Hill Cottage, preparing to settle down, when a commotion in the barn attracted his attention. Why the stableman wasn't available on that particular night remains unclear. It was important for Welton to discern what was causing the clamor, so he walked down the path to the horse stalls alone. Sure enough, two of his prize horses had somehow gotten loose and tangled themselves in the barn. They were tussling and biting each other, and Welton was about to separate the animals when one of the horses gave him a terrible kick. The servants immediately announced it was one of Mr. Welton's own favorites that injured him. That hoof-strike broke Welton's ribs and collapsed a lung. The injury was very bad—so bad in fact, that Joseph Chauncey Welton never did recover. He died five days later on March 26, 1874.

Directly following the funeral, people began talking, saying that it wasn't Welton's horse at all that killed him, but it was Carrie's stallion Knight that initiated the horrendous deed. Gossip circulated that Knight kicked Old Man Welton in the side of the head, and that's what caused the wealthy industrialist's demise.

Shortly thereafter, a different rumor made its way around Waterbury. Those damning whispers stated that it wasn't a horse that killed Mr. Welton, but it was actually Carrie who murdered her own father.[10] Folks said that Carrie planned it all, lured her father down to the stall and then used a shovel to bash Welton's skull. That's why the stable hand was absent that night; he was sent away on purpose. Whatever took place in that barn, it was Knight that ended up being blamed, and that horse was held responsible for the killing of Mr. Welton. The horse became the talk of all the Naugatuck Valley. Carrie was heartbroken. Not about her father's death—she was devastated when Knight passed away a year or so later, in 1875 or 1876. She buried Knight with expensive blankets for a shroud.[11] She could never discuss Knight afterward without becoming so overwrought as to swoon into a fit. Whenever her father's name happened to be mentioned, Carrie's whole expression would just glaze over—her eyes stared wide and looked far-faraway.

After Joseph Welton's death, money went to his immediate family, but the estate—the mansion and property—were divided in an odd way: they were divvied between his wife and daughter. Carrie got Rose Hill Cottage while her mother, Jane, inherited the grounds. This arrangement may have been what sparked their dour relationship. Carrie began locking herself away in her Rose Hill bedroom, staying sequestered for days upon days just to avoid her mother. After Carrie and Mrs. Welton returned from a West Coast excursion, Carrie got even worse. She went about blaming her mother for stealing things from around the mansion and inventing stories, saying that Jane Welton was walking about the house naked and carrying on improperly with all sorts of different men. Most bizarre was Carrie's intense fear of her mother, whom she accused of becoming a degenerate opium-eater. Carrie became adamant about her mother trying to poison her, too. Carrie told friends she'd find powder inside oranges and other fruit and that she also saw strange residue in her drinking glasses. Carrie became obsessed and studied books about strychnine, arsenic and all sorts of poisons. She exclaimed that her mother was dosing the house's drinking water with some kind of deadly potion. Carrie felt safe only by imbibing from the water buckets she had hoarded in her own locked bedroom.

Jane Welton was beside herself and finally called medical men to come check on her daughter. Drs. Charles McBurney and George Peters, alienists from New York City's insane asylum, drove up the driveway and knocked on the front door. They came to take Miss Carrie away, but after interviewing her, the two doctors saw no reason to incarcerate the girl.[12]

During her times of madness, poor Carrie took to referring to Rose Hill Cottage by a frightfully odd name: Echo Hill. Whether Carrie imagined she was hearing evil-intentioned whispers from her mother and servants or Carrie was taking directions from voices echoing in her head, not a single person could explain. Her behavior became more erratic, and Carrie took to sleeping with a pistol under her pillow. She even ran away at one point to stay with a friend. But Carrie acted just as strangely at her friend's house, hiding in the bedroom in the same manner as she was isolating herself at Rose Hill Cottage. Her friend expressed how unnervingly eerie it was the way Carrie would constantly sing monotone, nonsensical words and odd phrases for hours at a time behind her locked bedroom door. The whole household heard these awful chants. All the while, Carrie never stopped complaining about her mother trying to poison her. Then, on a whim, in 1880, Carrie Welton gathered her belongings and left Waterbury. She would never see Rose Hill Cottage again. At least not during her lifetime.

PART THREE: THE WEIRD, WEIRD WEST

By 1884, Carrie was roaming across the West, wandering the wildest places the country could offer. She fell in love with Colorado, especially the mountains. Mountain climbing gave Carrie the freedom she'd always been chasing. When she ascended Pike's Pike, Carrie witnessed an entrancing sight looming in the distance: Longs Peak. It was as if that mountain was personally calling out to Miss Welton, and she immediately decided to conquer that summit.

It was late September 1884 when Carrie decided to challenge this peak by hiring the guide, Carlyle Lamb. The Lamb family's livelihood centered on the wilderness surrounding Longs Peak. Carlyle's father, Elkanah, was an itinerate preacher who came out West, finally settling in Colorado. Elkanah was the first official trail guide in the Longs Peak area. When his nineteen-year-old son took over the hiking operation, the father tended to the business of running a mountain lodge for tourists.

On September 23, 1884, Carrie grabbed her pink domino mask, and with Carlyle Lamb beside her, together they set out for the top of the mountain. The pair got a late start on horseback, and it took them five hours to travel merely six miles. Finally, leaving the horses tied to some scrub trees, they set off on foot. The guide told Carrie that they should be coming down off the peak by this time of day instead of heading upward toward the summit. But Carrie would hear none of it. With an ominous sky gathering overhead,

Longs Peak, Colorado. The tragic wilderness death of Carrie Welton on this mountain during 1884 set in motion a litany of ghost stories. *Author's collection.*

Carlyle constantly warned Carrie that should they even make it to the higher elevation she sought, the heavy cloud cover would ruin any possible vista. Always a stubborn lass, Carrie rebuffed the guide and scolded him, "I have never undertaken anything and given it up."[13] The two hikers finally ascended the summit and rapidly turned around. But it was far too late in the day, and the storm that had been gathering had now transformed into a blizzard, one of the worst ever experienced. Carrie and Carlyle struggled down the mountain as far as humanly possible, but miles remained in front of them even before getting back to their horses—let alone the ranch. Carrie was already fainting from overexertion, while Carlyle's own strength was sapped from carrying the forty-two-year-old-woman down the mountainside. It was all too much for either of them. With each step, the brave hikers were flung backward and knocked down by the frigid blasts and raging snow. The guide and Carrie were forced to finally give up this futility. Shouting in each other's faces in order to be heard above the howling winds, they decided the

The desolate spot on Longs Peak where the frozen body of Waterbury's intrepid mountain climber and animal lover Carrie Welton was discovered. The wooden marker reads: "HERE Carrie Welton Lay to Rest. Died Alone Sept. 23, 1884." *Stiffler, George W., A grave believed to be near Silver Plume (1884–1892). Denver Public Library Digital Collections, accessed 1/11/2025, https://digital.denverlibrary.org/nodes/view/1102267.*

best course of action was for Carrie to remain behind while Carlyle forged onward for help. The guide huddled Carrie under a rock outcropping and built a snow shelter for her protection.

Carlyle battled the elements for hours before he finally reached his family's lodge and announced their deadly predicament. Even in robust physical condition, the young guide barely survived. Elkanah and his son set back out immediately to rescue Carrie. They found the woman on the trail, not far from the temporary shelter. Carrie had not waited but instead set out on her own. Poor Carrie had stumbled over snow-hidden rocks and, falling face downward, hit her head and lay unconscious, where she froze to death. The sight of her stiffened body was rendered surreal, as they discovered Carrie still wearing the pink domino mask she loved. It was a terrible fate for such a beautiful lady. Carrie Welton was the first recorded person to perish on Longs Peak. Weeks later, her funeral was held at Rose Hill Cottage. However, the tragic story does not end here.

Strangely enough, another weird aspect was added to Carrie's tragic tale in the form of an odd newspaper article. Front pages across the nation were emblazoned with the headline: "The Blizzard." But there was something very unnatural about the original report concerning Carrie and that monster storm. Newspaper readers certainly must have made a wide-eyed double-take at that particular column's dateline. Because "The Blizzard" article written about Carrie Welton, yes, "Miss Carrie Welton," appeared in print nine months prior to the actual calamity in which Carrie died. It was just another example of bizarre things dogging the occupants of Rose Hill Cottage, even into the afterlife. Whoever had written "The Blizzard" must have been a fortune-teller! The story that was printed well before Carrie froze to death was merely a romanticized fiction. An anonymous writer had randomly plucked a quaint sounding name, "Carrie Welton," while penning "The Blizzard." The make-believe "Carrie Welton" lived happily ever after with her loving beau, while the demise of the real-life Miss Welton generated much more frightful newspaper ink. It spelled out a wagon-full of trouble for that poor young trail guide.

In the weeks following Welton's doomed climb, Carlyle Lamb was crushed under an emotional avalanche. Not only was the guide devastated by the death of his female ward, but he also lay physically pummeled from the stormy excursion down the trail and the return-rescue attempt back up the mountain. Public opinion held that to save his own life Carlyle ran off and abandoned Carrie.[14] People said that the nineteen-year-old coward left Miss Welton to die alone on the mountain. An endless parade of journalists marched to Elkanah's guesthouse, situated at the base of Longs Peak, looking for witnesses. The old reverend sent his family away for the winter, far from those finger-pointing gawkers. Elkanah remained behind in order to finish work on guest cabins he'd already commenced building a month previous.[15]

During the first night of his family's absence, while the reverend worked alone at the lodge, something unexplainable occurred. Exhausted from the day's carpentry, Elkanah was in a deep sleep. Suddenly he found himself awakened by a fierce wind bearing down the mountainside. Gales swooped out of the behemoth crags above the lodge and hammered on the clapboards of that lonely place. For all the world, it sounded like someone banging on the outside walls trying to get at the reverend inside. Peering uneasily from under his bedsheets into the chamber's darkness, Elkanah's vision focused on the rattling window. There, just beyond the panes stood a figure, or so Elkanah thought; the misty outline slowly metamorphosed into a pale and wild-haired woman. The ghost's fingernails slowly scratched across the midnight glass. Elkanah snapped bolt upright in bed, fixated on the thing looming just a few feet away. The reverend recognized the wretched creature as Carrie Welton, "seemingly as natural as life."[16] That frightening visitation was recorded by Elkanah:

> *I am not superstitious and I do not believe in ghosts, spooks, or hobgoblins, but this ghostly appearance in the solitude of my lonely situation was the severest test of my mental equilibrium and courage ever before experienced in my life. Even while I was denouncing my superstitions, fears and feelings, a strange inexplicable fascination drew my eyes towards the window again, and there she stood gazing steadily towards me.*[17]

Never again did Elkanah Lamb suffer Miss Welton's supernatural wrath. However, events would prove that Carrie's ghostly Colorado manifestation was merely the first of a paranormal onslaught that would ensnare Rose Hill Cottage.

Part Four: Trapped Inside Rose Hill Cottage. Forever.

Being the sole owner of the Rose Hill mansion, when Carrie turned away from her mother and departed Waterbury for the West, the big house was again abandoned. Dark and lonely the foreboding hillside manor gazed down on the city, just as it did years earlier after the Scovills had died. If there had been any previous doubt about hauntings, Carrie's death now generated persistent rumors that the mansion was definitely full of ghosts.[18] From Prospect Street, individuals were always pointing out strange shadow

Beyond the Gates. Looming over Prospect Hill, historic Rose Hill Cottage owns a fascinating and macabre history. *Photograph by Michael J. Bielawa, taken May 27, 2022.*

figures seen flitting behind the curtains. In addition to Carrie, one of those frightful spirits supposedly included Joseph Welton. Carrie's murdered father roamed Rose Hill Cottage seeking revenge. There was a cavalcade of scary incidents. After Carrie Welton's passing, the hired help continued to check on the place. Shocked caretakers visiting the mansion swore that the doorknobs were covered with blood.[19] The large glass handles were wiped completely clean every time the strange red liquid was found congealing over the knobs. Inexplicably, the next morning the dripping blood reappeared. It became a common practice around this time for people strolling along Prospect Street to cross to the other side of the road when they approached Rose Hill Cottage.[20]

But it wasn't only the eerie house that people thought was haunted; the grounds surrounding the mansion were supposedly wraith-plagued as well. There were claims that Carrie's earthbound spirit was seen riding her beloved ghost stallion Knight during the wee hours. Many reported

Shrine to Carrie's True Love? Built with funds bequeathed by Carrie Welton and dedicated in 1888, the Welton Fountain is crowned with the bronze likeness of Carrie's stallion, Knight. Boldly located on Waterbury Green, the monument created a scandal, as this horse was rumored to be responsible for the death of Carrie's father. *Photograph by Michael J. Bielawa, taken May 27, 2022.*

Bronze or Ectoplasm? The ghost of this horse reportedly races along Waterbury's Hillside neighborhood. *Photograph by Michael J. Bielawa.*

hearing the terrifying disembodied sound of Carrie's laughter along with the plodding of invisible hooves. Some even stated that these two spirits had the power to escape the mansion's gated perimeter and were witnessed wandering up and down Prospect Street. Newspapers around the country continually reported about these worrisome occurrences. Locally, the paranormal reality remained firmly planted in the minds of everyone in Waterbury: ghosts stalked Rose Hill Cottage and its property.[21]

Surprisingly, Rose Hill Cottage remained empty for only a short while. But things inside the house were not quite normal. A continual parade of renters moved in and then just as quickly they raced out, spooked by whatever malevolent force existed inside the manor.[22] Many left their furniture behind. Some mornings the mansion's overseers would discover half-eaten meals on kitchen plates, the food abandoned as if the occupants had fled in a hurry. Even though these Waterbury ghosts were a viable topic of conversation across the county, the spirits didn't dissuade the curious from wanting to own Rose Hill Cottage. One woman, Martha Proper, who was living in the Dakota Territory at the time, made a bid to buy the mansion. Mrs. Proper, it was believed, thought that residing in a haunted house was less dangerous than living in the Dakota wilds.[23]

In 1888, Judge Edward Cole acquired the empty mansion. This happened to be the same year that Carrie Welton's final, and some believed most bold, eccentricity came to stride across Waterbury's Green. In her last will and testament, Carrie had set aside $7,000 for a water fountain and bronze equestrian statue featuring her beloved horse, Knight.[24] More than a few citizens guffawed when it was learned that the statue honored the memory of the animal that was rumored to have killed her father, Joseph Chauncey Welton.

However, the remaining Welton clan became truly incensed when they discovered that Carrie had bequeathed her entire inheritance to the Society for the Prevention of Cruelty to Animals. Her mother, Jane, her cousins and some other extended family all claimed Carrie was not in her right mind and sued in court to dissolve Carrie's wishes. During the legal proceedings of 1884–87, when the Welton family attempted, and failed, to dispose of

Day After Day Alone on a Hill. The Hillside neighborhood mansion and its apparitions have witnessed Waterbury's cityscape rise up around Rose Hill Cottage. *Photograph by Michael J. Bielawa, taken May 27, 2022.*

Carrie's will, Alexander Dallas, the gardener, testified that he thought Miss Welton was of sound mind.[25]

During the brief time in which Judge Cole had possession of Rose Hill Cottage, he rented the mansion to Anna Chase Whiting. She opened Rose Hill Cottage as a boardinghouse. Then in 1889, industrialist Augustus Chase purchased the home. The Chase family would continue to live in Rose Hill Cottage for nearly a century. The last Chase family member to own the Rose Hill home was Lucia Hosmer Chase, the world-recognized ballet dancer and founder of the American Ballet Theatre. Incidentally, Lucia Chase also used the Waterbury mansion as a retreat for ballet performers. Following the cultural icon's death in 1986, the old mansion witnessed major changes. Eventually, the rambling structure was acquired by the North American Family Institute/Stepping Stone in 1999 and served as a medium-security residential facility for incarcerated girls. In 2015, the City of Waterbury acquired the property for nearly $3 million. Virtually 170 years after William and Rebecca Scovill first envisioned a joyous life within their home's carved rose blossoms, the structure finally captured a renewed and benevolent bloom in 2019 when it became a community treasure as the administrative offices and annex building for the Greater Waterbury YMCA.

Dating back to the years before the American Civil War, Rose Hill Cottage has served as home to a vast array of far-flung Waterbury history. The mansion's ongoing story holds many strange and fascinating narratives. From the rich to the destitute. From ballet dancers to girls in juvenile detention. And perhaps, Rose Hill Cottage continues to be home to a brash female mountain climbing ghost.

3

WHO KNOCKS?

What am I doing here?
What am I doing here?
Tenderly bury the fair young dead,
Place a wooden cross at [her] *head…*
All the words you can say have been said
It's for you my tears are shed…
—Justin Hayward, The Moody Blues, "What Am I Doing Here?"

You've got to pick up every stitch.
—Donovan, "Season of the Witch"

The knock came again, its hollow thud forlorn as a clod of earth shoveled onto a coffin lid. Even now in the wee hours of the Ansonia night, the wretched sound had been anticipated. A desolate summons at the front door. Its call reverberated through the walls of the large Riverside Avenue house and slithered clammily across the skin of the Ryan family domiciled within. Huddled in their disarrayed Victorian parlor, the gas lamps burned bright, but the hissing glare did little to alleviate the darkness conveyed in each resounding bang at the door. The nightly knocking sound pulverized the already frayed nerves of the Ryan clan. Franticly, the family tossed and kicked inside their pell-mell temporary bedding. Patrick, the father, sprawled across the room's too small and stiff divan while his wife, Jane, uncomfortably sank deeper into the over-plush couch. Nearby, curled on the intricately patterned red and purple

Don't Answer the Door! Still from Murnau's *Nosferatu. Directed by F.W. Murnau, Prana Film, 1922.*

tasseled carpet, lay their youngest. Not even the lamps' gleam lessened the parlor's gloom. Putrid was the infernal darkness that accompanied the knock. The nightly knock.

When the knocking sound repeated, father, mother and child twisted out from their blankets and cautiously approached the front door. It had been two sleepless nights since the knocking commenced. Two nights. Two nights of knocking. When would it end?

Flopping dull and meaty against the front door, the noise startled the wide-eyed family each time it relentlessly landed. Again and again, their bare feet bounced on the floor. It wasn't only the Ryans inside their shattered Riverside Avenue abode who were glaring at that door. Folks up and down the street had come to expect the nocturnal arrival of the gruesome sound. But it was the visitor beyond the door that drove the Ryans and their neighbors to the brink of insanity. The nightly visitor. Now, two nights in a row. Two nights of this unworldly visitor. The entire neighborhood went without decent slumber. Frightened women with trembling hands brushed aside lace curtains, the better to scrutinize the queer thing standing on the Ryan's veranda. From the steps of their own adjacent porches, bold and bearded, adorned in calf-length nightgowns (some bareheaded, others topped with their workaday black derbies) neighbors peered into the night with knitted brows trying to make sense of the thing that knocked.

The clip-clop of a horse-drawn bakery wagon meandered down Riverside Avenue, the dray's beast lifting its head and snorting in response to something peculiar about the night. The driver, now alarmed, tilted his gaze toward the odd figure wavering on the porch. There was no need for the wagoner to snap the reins. The horse bounded forward, bouncing the cart down the street and leaving a trail of upset baked goods in its wake.

The wagon's clatter was noticed inside the Ryan home, too, where husband and wife, Patrick and Jane, moved deeper into the main hall. They were violently gesticulating the sign of the cross in front of the frosted-glass of their oaken door. Somehow, they were half hoping that tonight's knocking was a vexing hallucination prompted by tragic recent events. But they knew better. The thing had returned. Nauseating fear gripped the middle-aged Irish couple. Beyond the door's opaque façade loomed the ever-so-slightly rocking silhouette. The slender shadow was undeniably feminine. Jane approached the heavily bolted entrance and gripped a large chair wedged against the door; a sharp whisper burst from her pale lips, "What do you want?!" The only response was silence. The Ryan family stared and waited. The door window's paisley design framed the reticent phantasm. And then, another jarring knock.

Patrick's face contorted as he rasped a hushing command, "Woman. We can't just stand here a'worryin' about what she wants!"

Jane was at her wit's end; she shouted at her bewildered husband, "An' what do you want to do, Patrick Ryan? Let her in?! We know it's Jeannie. Our own flesh and blood! But we can'ot let the dead back in ta th' house. It's our home. A house for the living."

Patrick demanded, "Open the door. Open the door, or I will." His palsied hands dragged the heavy chair aside. Only glass and oak stood between the family and the entity. Patrick slowly twisted the deadbolt and then turned the brass doorknob…

FORTY-EIGHT HOURS EARLIER

On Saturday evening, February 13, 1886, Jeannie Ryan died.[1] Doctors, for some months prior, shook their heads at the inevitable outcome. "Heart disease," they somberly intoned, "No cure."

Across Connecticut, while Jeannie lay prostrate on her deathbed, that same day was memorable for an expressly different reason. The rains of the past week had finally ceased. The state had witnessed extreme flooding: roads and buildings had been swept away. And now, on the day of Jeannie's death, the sun and blue skies caressed the Naugatuck Valley. "How turr-able ironic," remarked the neighborhood's Gaelic community. The pretty twenty-one-year-old had been very popular, with a large circle of dear friends. The funeral, as expected, was a crowded and mournful affair fraught with wails and shrieks. Those gathered lamented how the spry lass had been a true credit to her upstanding parents.

After the solemn mass, mourners on the steps of Ansonia's Catholic Church commented how the poor wee corpse of Jeannie was being sent off to heaven in such a comely dress. A dress befitting a vibrant, noble soul. A dress created with the adoring hands of her mother, aided by the nimble fingers of neighboring womenfolk. A gown stitched together with sanctity and love. A gown appropriate to meet Saint Patrick, himself.

On Monday, February 15, 1886, the funeral cortege left the church for the final heart-tugging journey through Ansonia's streets. Black-plumed horses pulling the lacquered hearse struggled several times for proper footing in the deep mud.[2] Finally, the procession arrived at the tiny Irish burial yard.

But the sad drama of Jennie's passing would tragically magnify. On the same night that the young lady was buried, the Ryan household, palpably weighed down by morose sobs, found themselves jolted from their sorrowful brooding. It was that very night, the night of September 15, when the knocking commenced.

At daybreak, when the entity dematerialized, a wizened member from the neighborhood, an ancient dame with long white hair, braided and swirled atop her head, hobbled to the Ryan's succor. Her name, removed from memory, kindled tales of old cunning ways in Ireland. She explained to the shocked Ryan family that their daughter Jeannie slept a sleepless sleep in her grave. Invited into the parlor, the crone lowered herself into a wingback chair (the same piece of furniture that would soon be employed as a wedge for the front door). Resting arthritic-gnarled hands atop an ornate cane, the fey woman related, "Young Jeannie's visits will continue. Her wandering soul haunts you true; and this wraith will remain at your door until you die." According to tradition, explained the wrinkled seer, this haunting was compelled by a well-known curse, "Pins or wee knots accidently tucked amidst poor Jeannie's coffin-raiment's. Even a single knot at the end of a thread will condemn the soul to wander." Patrick and Jane stared in disbelief at the woman and then incredulously at each other. The old crone whispered, "Those guilty o' the blunder shall be forever disturbed by this anxious spirit."[3]

The Ryans blanched at the bizarre notion. Aghast, they skeptically shrugged off such a supernatural diagnosis. That is, until Jeannie's second night of knocking. Now the whole street listened and watched and begged the Ryan clan to act.

ON THE THIRD DAY FOLLOWING THE BURIAL

After dragging the wedged chair off to the side, Patrick Ryan did not open the front door on this night. The moment he grabbed the brass knob, Jane gripped his shoulder. Her words were curt: "No. Don't open the door….It's time we go a-visiting Jeannie."

Later that morning, a newspaperman out of New Haven caught wind about an Irish corpse's nocturnal forays. Calculating that the astounding Ansonia gossip could provide readers with a fanciful tall-tale, the scribe headed northward into the Naugatuck Valley. He never reached the Ryan home—instead he found himself detoured behind a procession of four women, one of whom was Jane, the deceased girl's mother. The weird assemblage was heading for the Irish cemetery. Entering through a side gate, the women, accompanied by the reporter, encircled a fresh earthen mound of the newly buried.

According to the February 18, 1886 *New Haven Evening Register*, "Presently two men made their appearance and with shovels, opened the grave. The women stood with bated breath, tears running down their faces." Hushed expressions measured the shovelfuls of dirt exiting the pit. When a spade struck the oblong box, "One of the women gave a low scream." The sextons tossed their tools out of the yawning grave and turned their attention to wrestling the coffin aboveground. The newspaper article continued, "The lid was taken off the box and the casket opened. The features of a young handsome and beloved daughter of one of the women was exposed to view. The men [surely including the dazed reporter] looked on as if in wonder [at] what followed."[4]

Hunching forward, the ladies reached into the coffin. Grabbing poor Jeannie's gown and bunching it in their wrinkled hands the group frantically searched for an overlooked knot or misplaced pin. Silky material hissed between their luridly hunting fingers. Reverently, Jeannie's lifeless head was raised and cradled from behind by one person while another scoured the dead girl's hair just in case a pin lay hidden in her long locks. Probing the clothes that encased Jeannie's body, one of the elderly ladies let out a startled yelp. A pin! The occult source of Jeannie's hideous knockings pierced one of the elderly ladies' wrinkled fingers in the same mundane manner any seamstress might stumble onto an errant needle. The tiny metal culprit was held aloft for all to witness. The old woman brought her punctured finger toward her lips but paused, deciding it might not be prudent to lick a dab of blood from a pin resting in a haunted grave.

Later, the women all whisperingly attested that when the offending object had been removed, they all heard a sigh rising from the open coffin. Though they weren't exactly positive, they noticed too that Jeannie's lips twitched ever so slightly into a momentary grin.

The *New York Herald*, dated February 19, 1886, published an account of the Ansonia occurrences. The article noted, "All the pins that had been used to hold the cerements in place were removed and carefully treasured. The string with which the feet were tied together was taken away. Then one of the women took a needle and thread, and where pins had been removed stiches were taken, care being had that no knots were tied in the thread. After the operation was concluded the women signaled to the men that the coffin was again to be interred." While brushing the dank scent of coffin from her hands, one of the women stated, "Now that the duty is done to the dead, the living are all happy and all will be peace."[5]

Shrouded within the morning's cold sunlight, wearily but satisfied, Jeannie's mother gazed on the refilled grave. She held a single pin in her grip. It pierced her palm. A drop of blood fell. The red speck landed on the freshly pounded mound of earth like a miniature clod of dirt shoveled onto a coffin lid. Unlike the unnatural knocking at her family's front door, it was the quietest of sounds happily unheard.

However, the tale is not over. Additional odd events might be in the offing, thus compelling further research. The disinterment of Jeannie Ryan's Ansonia grave provided a tantalizing, and unnerving, statement found in the *New Haven Evening Register*'s 1886 coverage: "This is not the first time that an incident of the kind [a search for pins and knots within a grave] has occurred in the same cemetery."[6] What other ancestors might come knocking on the front doors of their family's Naugatuck Valley homes?

4
The Midnight Watchman

I am the midnight watchman.... I watch the metal rusting,
and I watch the time go by.
—Harry Chapin, "A Better Place to Be"

It was nearly midnight, and Robert Dover stood alone in the vast courtyard of Wallace & Son's factory,[1] intently gazing up at the plant's tallest smokestack. As had been his nightly routine during the past few months, the brass mill's newest security guard was synchronizing his pocket watch while patiently awaiting the smokestack to strike twelve—indeed, a huge clock was embedded halfway up the smokestack's brick façade. In a few moments, the Ansonia landmark would call out the witching hour.[2] Satisfied that the ticking hands of his pocket watch matched the clanking arms of the giant overhead, Dover closed the brass cover of his timepiece and proceeded through the massive interior doors of the foundry. It was now midnight and time for another security check. During this late hour, access to the sprawling complex was limited to the merest skeleton crew of two guards. The cacophony of whirring and pounding machines had been silenced two hours earlier, at ten o'clock, thus making for a tranquil walk throughout the plant. But his rounds would be far from peaceful: Robert Dover had no idea just how far his steps would carry him into the realm of the macabre.

Meandering through the machinery-choked labyrinth of one of the factory's expansive buildings, the truncheon-twirler was suddenly gripped by an unsettling feeling. Something was wrong, very wrong. The source of Dover's consternation turned out to be Emil Fritz. Old Fritz was a longtime guard at Wallace & Son's. And as was Emil's nocturnal habit, there he was, planted in his usual spot, perched reflectively on a wooden chair near the engine room enjoying a cigarette. Emil always unintentionally managed to annoy Dover with just a smile. That's because Emil never displayed a worry in the world, which is what bothered the new full-timer most of all: Fritz just sitting there, smoking and smiling. But this scene was far from normal. The new guard couldn't make a shred of sense out of what was transpiring before his eyes. All Dover knew was that Emil Fritz shouldn't have been working this midnight shift. Or any shift. Emil Fritz was dead.[3] Emil Fritz had been dead nearly four months. Dover started to approach his colleague but inadvertently paused with a shudder. The oak chair beneath Emil creaked loudly as he tilted it back against the wall. Turning his head ever so slowly toward Dover, Emil's pale countenance creased into a gruesome rictus. The new watchman's eyes went wide. With his free hand, Dover reached for his holstered sidearm while backing away from Emil, who merely continued to smile. Unable to look away from the seated guard, Dover stumbled through the factory and finally burst out of a side exit. He

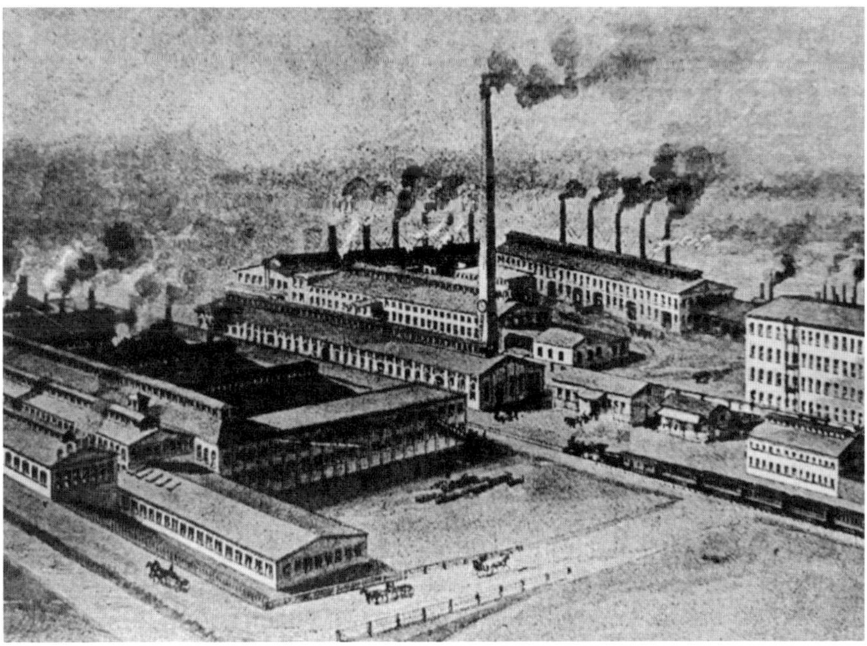

Wallace & Sons Factory. The nineteenth-century brass manufacturer was supposedly haunted. The immense clock built into the tallest smokestack was a Naugatuck Valley landmark. There's a ladder leaning against the smokestack to facilitate changing the clock's hands. *From* Town and City Atlas of the State of Connecticut, *D.H. Hurd & Co., 1893.*

voraciously gulped the damp night air. Catching his breath, the stunned guard took some solace leaning against the mill's giant smokestack, while overhead the familiar sounds of the huge clock helped settle Dover's racing nerves. With trembling fingers, the guard rebuttoned the safety strap over the top of his revolver. Robert Dover realized that he had come face to face with the ghost of Emil Fritz.

Records indicate that Emil Fritz had worked as a night watchman at the brass mill for at least six years, dating to 1880. The German immigrant, according to the February 24, 1886 *Derby Transcript*, was known as a "faithful employee…[and had] always been considered sober and industrious." His social circle included a number of friends, and Emil enjoyed membership in the local George Washington Masonic lodge.[4] The thirty-eight-year-old lived with his southern-born wife, Caroline, and their three children: Gertrude, Charles and an unnamed toddler. The family resided on Winter Street in Ansonia, just a short walk for Emil to his nightly job.[5]

The hair-raising materialization of Emil Fritz's phantom as witnessed by Robert Dover, occurred on Sunday, June 6, 1886. But this was only the first paranormal incident that would be reported by the mill's security crew. Several days after Fritz's ghostly arrival, Robert Dover was once again conducting his midnight rounds. Entering a cavernous portion of the factory, the guard heard the unmistakable sound of rattling chains. The groan of jangling metal was emanating from the far side of the building. Dover immediately envisioned Emil taking on the ghastly shape of Jacob Marley's ghost in Dickens' *Christmas Carol*, but instead of wandering through a dreary London mansion, Emil was here, now, in this very factory angrily dragging a length of shackles across the floor. Hesitantly, Dover approached the jarring sound, determined to investigate its source.

He exhaled, relieved.

Dover's eyes caught sight of a long stretch of heavy chain swirling from a high ceiling crane. He walked toward the spinning iron dervish looking to see who was inside the crane's enclosed control room. Obviously, so Dover thought, another guard on duty must be operating the machinery. But as Robert Dover got within full view of the crane's controls, he discovered that nobody was manipulating the levers.[6]

Confused, the guard proceeded down the hall, where he entered the engine room. Here, Dover found the factory's sole other guard squatting in front of an enormous motor. The fellow gazed up from his toolkit and greeted Robert Dover. "Who," Dover exclaimed, "is operating the crane?"

Stuffing a rag into his back pocket as he stood up, the second guard explained that he'd been cleaning the gears and gauges in this room for at least an hour. Dover inquired if his coworker had been near the crane at any time during the evening? He replied in the negative. The two men exchanged alarmed glances. Apparently, there was an intruder in the factory. Together they returned to the crane's gyrating chain. However, the machinery was now powered down; everything was absolutely normal. Unnerved by the inexplicable event, Dover confessed to his partner that he'd seen the ghost of Emil Fritz on the previous Sunday.

The foundation for these strange occurrences began four months earlier. When Emil Fritz left work near dawn on Friday, February 19, 1886, the night watchman clutched his lunch bucket and exited the gates of Wallace & Son's. That same morning, Emil escorted a relative to the Ansonia train station. Afterward, he walked home to his second-floor flat on Winter Street, where he lay down for a nap. Unable to sleep, Emil got up from bed at two o'clock in the afternoon. He joined his wife, Carrie, in the kitchen, where he casually lit a cigarette (a habit of which his spouse angrily disapproved). A shouting match resulted. Mrs. Fritz stormed off into the apartment's front room. The apartment assumed an uncomfortable quiet until about an hour later, at approximately three o'clock, when a loud popping sound disrupted the uneasy silence. Mrs. Fritz thought it resembled a window blind snapping shut, while her nine-year-old daughter, Gertrude, remarked how much the noise seemed like a gunshot.[7]

Carrie ran to check on her husband and discovered Emil was bloodied and stretched across their bed. "What have you done?" she venomously spat.

The wounded man gasped, "I've shot myself. Send for Doctor Welch!"[8] Those were Emil's last words. Before help arrived, the watchman was dead.

Dr. William Collin Welch had been a friend of Emil's.[9] The physician had initially become acquainted with the factory worker while treating

Fritz for depression, a condition all too casually dismissed during this era as "nervous troubles."[10]

When Dr. Welch's ministrations failed to revive the prostrate and blood-soaked Emil, the Yale medical school graduate summoned Dr. George L. Beardsley. Beardsley had been practicing medicine in Derby for eleven years, and just six months earlier, he had assumed what would become his longtime career as the local medical examiner.[11]

Surveying the Fritzes' bedroom, the ME located evidence he was already seeing far too frequently in his new job as forensic specialist. Dr. Beardsley's investigations into the homes of overworked, underpaid and emotionally wrought laborers led to a repeatedly tragic prognosis: suicide.

From the evidence he gathered, Beardsley surmised that Emil had braced his back against the bedroom's closet door, raised a revolver to his heart (just above the left nipple) and pulled the trigger. The bullet entered Emil's chest, exited the body and continued a trajectory through the closet's door, where it finally bounced off the tiny room's back wall. As proof, a slightly dented slug was found on the closet floor. Dr. Beardsley scanned the bedroom, mentally re-creating how Emil fired the pistol and then proceeded to stumble five feet away from the closet and collapse onto the bed where his wife discovered him. A gun lay on the quilt next to the dead man. The five-shot Smith & Wesson pistol would later be identified as the same weapon Emil carried on his job at Wallace & Son's. A quick analysis confirmed that a single cartridge within the gun's barrel had been fired.

What the doctors and authorities deemed an obvious case of suicide was soundly refuted by a skeptical public. Neighbors sensed something was amiss about the guard's demise. Within seventy-two hours, circumstances surrounding Emil's final desperate act began to generate unsettling questions. First, there was the immaculate bullet. Strangely, the .32-caliber projectile Dr. Beardsley recovered from the closet floor was unstained. There was no evidence of blood or body tissue on the slug. More damning, however, was the discovery of a second spent bullet.[12]

Emotionally scarred, Mrs. Fritz loathed entering the bedroom where her husband had taken his life. It wasn't until three days later, well after the room and mattress had been thoroughly examined by the medical personnel, that Carrie finally removed the gore-stained linens. Tossing one of the pillows toward the foot of the bed, the grieving widow distinctly heard a dull metallic thud. It turned out to be a second, and, in this instance, bloodied bullet. The projectile had been concealed deep inside a pillow's feathers and was exposed only when it clattered onto the wooden floor.

What followed has never been accurately explained. Authorities perpetuated an old-fashioned form of shell-game in which evidence was seemingly hidden. After an inquiring journalist made a straightforward request to inspect the two bullets side by side, Dr. Beardsley told him to go ask for Dr. Welch's assistance. The newspaperman did just that, approaching the Fritz family physician in the doctor's Main Street offices located within the Hotchkiss Block. Welch's staff then explained to the newspaperman that the doctor was out, having been summoned by the medical examiner, Dr. Beardsley. The reporter stated that he would wait for Welch's return. When Dr. Welch finally got back to the office, he nonchalantly explained to the journalist that the bullets were in the possession of the medical examiner.[13] It is unknown if the reporter ever got to examine the different slugs.

With the appearance of the second bullet, folks wondered aloud if an unknown assailant had, in fact, murdered Emil.[14] Even more shocking was the question of whether this violent act had been perpetrated by Mrs. Fritz? Long simmering animosity within the Fritz marriage had Ansonia gossips nodding. As soon as that second slug skidded across the bedroom floor, stories exploded around town about the Fritzes' volatile relationship. Neighbors reported that the loud argument between Emil and Carrie on that fateful day was an all-too-common occurrence.

Questions arose about the couple's ongoing bickering, Emil's supposed suicide and how a dead man could pull a trigger twice. As implausible as it might have sounded, Carrie suddenly remembered that her husband, blinded with anger during a recent rage, had raced into their bedroom to grab his pistol. Carrie explained that Emil fired a single shot into the closet, hoping to kill Carrie while she sat in an adjacent room. To support her story, Mrs. Fritz pointed out a bullet hole in the closet door that had been repaired. The authorities were skeptical at best, but Carrie's neighbors openly scoffed at the woman's wild account.

However, the fact remained that Emil's mental state had been fraught for some time by paranoid sentiments concerning his wife's involvement with another man. A few years prior, Fritz confided to his closest friends that when he had gone overseas to visit family, the German military forced the night watchman to complete the compulsory military service he'd previously evaded. Upon returning to America, he felt certain that during his absence Carrie had met a paramour. Proof of the illicit romance, in Emil's mind, were his wife's many excursions into New York City.[15] Mrs. Fritz brushed aside her husband's accusations, saying that her repeated Manhattan visits were merely an opportunity to be with her own family. Over time, these heated arguments exacerbated the watchman's "passionate and excitable nature," noted the *Derby Transcript*.[16] (Connecticut newspapers weren't the only outlets covering this potential murder mystery. Morbid fascination with Emil's death sparked interest well beyond the Naugatuck Valley. Newspaper subscribers devoured ongoing word of the tragedy as far away as Cleveland, Ohio.[17])

As for the supernatural events occurring inside Wallace & Son's, folks certainly must have scratched their heads over why Emil's spirit chose to haunt his workplace and not his Winter Street home? Was Fritz's ghost shadowing a particular individual in the factory? After Emil's burial, Robert Dover saw fit to move to Winter Street, just a few houses away from the widow Carrie Fritz.[18] Might it have been Dover to whom Carrie had been showing affection? If so, maybe Emil's wraith was hounding his wife's lover? Or perhaps Emil's unexplained appearances at the factory were the byproduct of Dover's overly imaginative guilty conscience. There was another intriguing fact added into the odd mix: part-time guard Robert Dover was hired full-time as a replacement for Emil Fritz. On a benevolent note, could it be that the spectral security guard was merely keeping a keen eye on Dover to ensure that the factory's midnight rounds were properly conducted?

As for Carrie and her children, they departed Ansonia in a matter of months after her husband's death. In 1888, she remarried in the exact place Emil complained that his wife was visiting too frequently: Manhattan.[19] The new Mrs. Cors would eventually live with her second husband, John, in New Jersey (John Cors would also die in an untimely manner near the end of the nineteenth century).

The twice-widowed Carrie was forced to take in sewing at her home in order to pay the bills. She passed away in the Bronx, alone, at age seventy-three, in October 1928. Her sparse thirty-three-word obituary listed no relatives. The death notice concluded: "Kindly omit flowers."[20]

As for the site of Emil's haunting, Wallace & Son's became insolvent during the economic Panic of 1893. It was acquired by Coe Brass Company in 1896, and then three years later, it was absorbed into the American Brass Company. Time also ran out for the giant smokestack and its celebrated timepiece that Robert Dover had always been attracted to. It was razed in 1917, just a few weeks prior to America's entry into the First World War. Unceremoniously, the massive clock's jumble of springs and gargantuan gears were carted off to the trash heap. Quite ironically, the next year and a half marked a period when clocks and calendars forever froze in homes across the United States memorializing American doughboys killed in European trenches.[21]

What was once the site of the vast and frenetic Wallace & Son's complex today broods mutely on the banks of the Naugatuck. The river's endless stream-song lulls these shores where once a legion of brass workers toiled. But it is not all quiet. As another midnight approaches and the invisible hands of a vanished smokestack's clock inch toward the witching hour, Emil Fritz might yet arrive. Summoned back to his favorite chair, reflectively smoking a cigarette, observing the metal rusting and smiling as time slips by.

5

Tales of the Bloody Hookman

Stories surrounding the Hookman and his connection with Great Hill Cemetery in Seymour, Connecticut, have terrified generations of Naugatuck Valley residents. Countless teens trading scary stories during slumber parties or around campfires have unleashed many sleepless nights due to this gory urban legend. The following chapter examines the various origins and themes associated with the Hookman as he has become known in the Naugatuck Valley. Those familiar with the tales surrounding the bloody Hookman's reign of terror recall hearing a variation of the following story and the harrowing experience of two anonymous teens.

The car turned off the heavily wooded Holbrook Road and veered onto desolate Cemetery Road. Once this narrow lane hosted the far more ancient sounding moniker of Burying Ground Road. But that was long before the car's driver and his passenger were even born. The road's eerie name is derived from the adjacent Great Hill Cemetery, whose earliest gravestones date to the late eighteenth century.

The car comes to a rumbling halt. There are no other vehicles nearby, and it's got to be at least a few hundred yards of tangled forest and dense brush camouflaging the nearest porch light. The lonely area around Great Hill Cemetery is a teenager's dream spot for romantic parking.

All is silent, except for the song of summer crickets filling the car. The boyfriend waits a long moment before awkwardly flopping an arm over his girlfriend's shoulders. Cool move, huh? The lothario congratulates himself.

But the girlfriend will have none of it.

She is too preoccupied about the stories she's heard at school. Stories about the Hookman lurking near the cemetery where they are parked. The gloomy cemetery just beyond the car's open window. The girl recalls the tale from a friend of a friend—a long time ago Mr. Hookman had been the caretaker right here at Great Hill Cemetery. Mr. Hookman was a mean old buzzard, and he didn't tolerate anyone invading his gravestone domain. So, when one wiseacre kid (on a dare) wandered into the hillside cemetery late one night, Mr. Hookman grabbed hold of him and dragged the boy over to a big tree, where he impaled the poor kid with a hook. The murderous cemetery caretaker left the boy dangling from that huge tree. Or, wait. Did the actual story say that the old cemetery groundskeeper had a hook for a hand? Yeah, that's it, the girlfriend nods to herself, the real story has the Hookman displaying a hook instead of a hand. She recalls hearing that the Hookman committed some unmentionably terrible crime. A vengeful mob swarmed the cemetery with the intent of teaching the Hookman a lesson. The frenzied crowd tracked down the

Lair of the Hookman. Great Hill Cemetery in Seymour, Connecticut, has a long connection to one of America's most bloody urban legends. *Photograph by Michael J. Bielawa, taken September 9, 2024.*

prosthetic wearing (but innocent?) caretaker and surprised him inside his ramshackle hut. The maddened throng hanged that man who had a hook for a hand. It was the Hookman who the mob left swaying from a tree just inside the cemetery wall. Another ending to this same story says that the man with the hook hand escaped the crazed mob's lynching. Supposedly he bolted off into the woods surrounding the cemetery. And it's that Hookman who still roams nearby, spying on couples who park near the cemetery.

But hold on a moment, there's yet another story. This one has the Hookman sadly taking his own life—tossing a rope over the limb of a big cemetery tree. It could have been the tree right here, the tree the boyfriend and girlfriend are parked under at this very moment.

Others testify that a long time ago there was a large family that lived in a broken-down cabin behind the burial grounds. The parents who lived in that decrepit hovel had a difficult time keeping an eye on their odd son. One night, the strange boy went berserk. He slaughtered his entire family. With a hook. Well, the story goes that it's this same weird boy who lurks in these woods. Some say that on each Halloween the cursed and long-lost house materializes out of the cemetery's fog—and that's when the boy-murderer returns with his hook seeking more victims. Another common motif has a deranged hook-adorned madman escaping from a psychiatric hospital and wandering lonely roads preying on teenagers.

It didn't matter which of the stories was true.[1] The girlfriend's only worry was that the Hookman was, indeed, somewhere out there. In the woods? Hiding behind the cemetery wall? Near the car? Getting closer? It's the reason why everyone, yes, everyone, in the Naugatuck Valley calls this graveyard Hookman's Cemetery.[2] And now, at this very moment, the girlfriend becomes certain that she heard something. She complains to her boyfriend. Breathlessly, she explains that it sounds like a kind of scratching noise. The boyfriend hears nothing. Wait, maybe there is something he heard, something familiar, but very faint? Yes, there is a noise! Something is scratching the car's roof. The girlfriend wonders aloud if the scraping sounds are coming from the hanged Hookman's heels that are dragging ever-so-slowly across the metallic roof? Or is the Hookman very much alive and using his metallic hand to taunt the teens by scratching the car's side panels?

The boyfriend isn't quite convinced. The night is young—but his girlfriend insists that they leave now.

The boyfriend turns the ignition key and presses on the gas pedal, his car roaring down the dark lane. Arriving in the girlfriend's driveway, he walks around to the other side of the car to open her door. The boyfriend freezes. His eyes bulge wide.

Caught in the car door handle is a dangling hook.

The morbid assortment of unnerving Hookman fables has been prevalent in the Naugatuck Valley dating back to the 1960s. But archetypes of the Hookman story were already ingrained in the American psyche for at least ten years prior. Mr. Hookman's bloody origin is often traced by sociologists and folklorists to two specific twentieth-century rampages that viciously targeted couples parking in isolated areas. The first of these true-life crimes occurred in 1946, when a series of lovers' lane murders occurred over a three-month period in the city of Texarkana.[3] The serial killer was never caught. These unsolved crimes inspired the 1976 film *The Town That Dreaded Sundown*.[4]

In October 1975, a year before the horror movie was released, Ansonia resident Carolyn (Barth) DeLieto had her own brush with the Hookman. Looking forward to membership in her high school sorority, fourteen-year-old Carolyn accepted an initiation challenge of being dropped off, alone, at night, at Hookman's Cemetery. "The senior girls drove a bunch of us up that creepy winding road," Carolyn recently reminisced. "I was terrified. It was dark, and they left me at the cemetery gate. I thought I heard all kinds of things, but it was probably just my imagination. I was standing there for maybe ten minutes when the car came back for me. We all had curfews at home and there were other girls waiting in the car to be dropped off individually, so they could face their own Hookman challenge." Carolyn happily reports that she did, indeed, pass the initiation.[5]

The second sinister source that's been attributed to unleashing the Hookman's dark legacy focuses on Caryl Chessman and his violent 1948 Los Angeles crime spree. The kidnapper and serial rapist attacked couples parking on Mulholland Drive and in West Pasadena, California. Arrested and convicted for these crimes, Chessman served nearly a dozen years on death row before being executed in San Quentin Prison's gas chamber in May 1960.[6]

Later that same year, the Hookman became a bona fide nationwide sensation. On November 8, 1960, the day Kennedy was elected president of the United States, Abigail Van Buren (her real name was Pauline Friedman Phillips), ran the following letter in her syndicated column, Dear Abby:

> *If you are interested in teenagers, you will print this story. I don't know whether it's true or not, but it doesn't matter because it served its purpose for me:*
>
> *A fellow and his date pulled into their favorite "lovers' lane" to listen to the radio and do a little necking. The music was interrupted by an announcer who said there was an escaped convict in that area who had served time for rape and robbery. He was described as having a hook instead of a right hand. The couple became frightened and drove away. When the boy took his girl home, he went around to open the car door for her. Then he saw—a hook on the door handle! I don't think I will ever park to make out as long as I live. I hope this does the same for other kids.* [The letter was signed,] *"Jeanette."*[7]

Odd as it might sound, the voyeur Hookman owes part of his sinister creation myth to America's changing attitudes toward sex. By the mid-twentieth century, with traditional sexual mores relaxing and the number of households owning cars expanding, combined with the urban population relocating to suburbia, these societal shifts had generated an opportunity for intimate roadside dalliances. And gave birth to the Hookman. Folklorists and sociologists explain that the terrifying situations initially produced by the Texarkana and Los Angeles crimes (mixed in with society's energized teen relationships) transmogrified into the cautionary tale we now recognize as the elusive, but ubiquitous, Hookman. The message is straightforward. Teenagers should not engage in "parking," i.e., having sex.[8]

Knowingly, or perhaps subconsciously, a warning motif was born in the shape of a metal claw that would dissuade young people, particularly girls, from parking with teen boys—either the story preemptively forestalled a hormonal adventure on an empty country road or unidentified scraping sounds prompted a very real and frightening reason to start the car and vacate the desolate spot.

It soon became apparent that an army of Hookmen would be needed to regularly escape the confines of far-flung mental institutions in order to derail the amorous intentions of America's ever-widening audience of teenagers impatiently nuzzling in the glow of dashboard lights. As such, stories of the frightening metal-appendaged killer migrated across the country during the 1960s, with the Hookman making appearances in Kansas, New Mexico, New Jersey, Utah, Maryland, Wisconsin, Indiana, Illinois, Texas, Arkansas, Oregon, California and Canada.[9] That's a lot of couples parking, not to mention tons of hooks scratching against car doors.

However, there are those familiar with Hookman's Cemetery in Seymour who feel certain that something far darker than an urban legend wanders this paranormal site. Former Oxford, Connecticut resident Aly Butler knows the area well, having lived for years near Great Hill Cemetery. Aly hiked through these woods as a youngster and shares a very different opinion about venturing into the thickets around Cemetery Road. "The area has a weird vibe; it is definitely one of the loneliest places I've ever known." Reflecting on her days growing up close to the burial grounds, Aly explained, "I'd hike those woods around the cemetery when I was a little kid," and with a shudder added, "Those woods are way creepier than the graveyard." Recollecting her early rambles, Aly continued, "Walking deep into the Great Hill woods, there are no trails, a person wandering there could hear… 'things.'" Aly paused and then added, "*things* that don't quite belong." When questioned about these weird noises, Aly replied, "There are sounds that don't belong in the woods. Remember, there are no houses or other buildings out there, but I could hear what sounded like doors creaking and groaning." Pausing to listen to her own vivid memories, Aly gazed into the distance, "I absolutely heard the sound of creaking doors. The invisible doors were near me. Opening on what sounded like old rusty hinges." Suddenly, Butler became unwilling to continue the conversation.[10]

Connecticut offers a dark autumn harvest of Hookman saunterings. Depending on whether one lives near Great Hill Cemetery or closer to the Rhode Island border, there exists two identical hook-gouging entities roaming the desolate backroads of this state. In addition to Hookman's Cemetery in Seymour, a rival hook-equipped night visitor hails from Montville's Black Ash Road in eastern Connecticut.[11] One surefire method to determine whose car door dangling hook is the drop-dead real deal requires only two adventurous keen-eyed couples to park along both these lonely roads under a moonless sky. Is it a date? The Hookman is waiting.

6

Occurrences in the Birmingham National Bank

A Tale of Two Vaults

The Coffins Needed a Home

The valley's landscape had been ravaged by the raging Naugatuck River one terrible August day in 1955. Afterward, as survivors sorted through whatever waterlogged remnants they could find where once their shattered homes and businesses and normal lives had previously stood, volunteers also found caskets that had been wrenched from their underground resting places. Sent plummeting helter-skelter downstream within the Naugatuck's debris-churning floodwaters, the far-flung remains would take months to locate. Naturally, the newly recovered bodies had to be temporarily housed somewhere. One of these interim morgues, according to Michael Picone, was situated in the basement of the downtown Derby, Connecticut Birmingham National Bank. The presence of these coffins, with their tragically displaced occupants, might explain the paranormal occurrences taking place in the Main Street building. Picone should know. He owns the Twisted Vine Restaurant, which is now located in the old bank. Due to the volume of unexplained incidents reported in this venue, the Twisted Vine is recognized as one of America's most haunted restaurants.

During Picone's two decades as owner of the Twisted Vine, customers have approached him to share their personal memories about the time when the bank was used as a makeshift morgue. Some people explained that they were related to bank employees who witnessed the bodies in the bank's cellar following the 1955 flood, while other individuals told Picone how they were involved with transporting bodies to and from the bank building after the floodwaters receded.[1]

Situated near the confluence of the Naugatuck and Housatonic Rivers, the Birmingham National Bank was constructed in 1892. Beautifully detailed, the Richardsonian Romanesque–style building was, and is, a glorious red sandstone and brick symbol celebrating Derby's Victorian heritage (during that time, the city was known as Birmingham). Another one of the bank's marvelous and unique features is the original main vault. The enormous doors were constructed of chrome, steel and brass,[2] and the bombproof recess possesses one of the world-renowned Diebold Safe & Lock Company's earliest lock serial numbers: 001. Imagine the valuable documents and family secrets that generations of Naugatuck Valley residents once secured inside safe-deposit boxes located within these massive walls. Now, this vault holds ghostly whispers.

And the Dead Shall Rise…in the Flood of 1955. The killer flood that ravaged the Naugatuck Valley did not even allow the dead to rest. The voracious currents scoured cemeteries and sent buried coffins churning downstream. Open graves and scattered casket vaults are pictured here in Seymour's Union Cemetery following the deadly flood. *From* Western Connecticut's Great Flood Disaster, August 19, 1955. *Booklet. The* Waterbury (Conn) Republican American, *1955. Courtesy of the* Waterbury Republican American.

Above: Birmingham Bank in 1896. Repurposed over the decades from a bank to a senior center to a popular restaurant, the building is noted for its ghostly activities. *From C.B. Gillespie,* Souvenir History of Derby and Shelton, Connecticut. *The Transcript Company, 1896.*

Opposite: A Tale of Two Vaults. The bank vault that Samuel Lessey unlocked and entered on a regular basis would soon be exchanged for a darker vault from which he'd never escape. *Photograph by Michael J. Bielawa, taken August 30, 2024.*

The Birmingham National Bank retained its old-charm name until the financial institution merged with the Home Trust Company and the Second National Bank of New Haven in early 1965. In 1971, the new bank's offices were moved out of the Victorian-era building and relocated to Elizabeth Street. During the disco era, the former bank building served as an adult education center until its slow fall from grace finally relegated the empty structure to nothing more than a pigeon roost. The forlorn Main Street icon squatted neglected and abandoned until it was rescued and rechristened in 1982 as the Olde Birmingham Restaurant. More recently, the repurposed building has hosted several Naugatuck Valley eateries, including the short-lived Reggio DiPuglia (about 1992), followed by the popular Tartaglia's restaurant (approximately 1993–2004), and now, since July 2005, the magnificent Twisted Vine Restaurant. The daily chalkboard specials at each of these bistros may have varied, but the one constant item on their set menu has been a regular serving of ghost stories.

John R. Fogerty worked here in 1987 when the place was known as the Olde Birmingham Restaurant. The sous chef recounts how waitresses would race into the kitchen in order to escape flying glassware. Fogerty explained how staff would "always come running into the kitchen frightened out of their minds; they were always seeing or hearing something freaky."[3] Over the years, workers have repeatedly witnessed drinking glasses set into motion by invisible hands and sent soaring across the dining area. The specters seem to delight in manipulating tableware as this form of poltergeist activity continues to this day.

When Black Barrel Records owner Nicholas Howard was a server in the restaurant during the 2013 holiday season, he related how, after arranging the balcony tables' dinnerware for the next days' business, a glass he'd just set down in the center of a table somehow went crashing to the floor. It was after hours, and no one was near the table.[4]

Olde Birmingham Restaurant. Beginning in the 1980s, the old bank building became a highly regarded Naugatuck Valley eatery. The tradition continues into the twenty-first century with the Twisted Vine Restaurant. The menu has changed, but the ghosts remain. *Advertisement originally appeared in* The Sunday Post *(Bridgeport, CT), November 22, 1987, Author's collection.*

Twisted Vine restaurateur Mike Picone and head waiter David Harmon have witnessed a litany of unexplainable incidents. Dave has worked in the building for three decades, having been employed by both Tartaglia's and the Twisted Vine restaurants (Picone states that Harmon is his invaluable "right hand man"). During his years here, David has experienced the bar's downstairs jukebox suddenly begin playing an old song even though no one is near the machine. Sweet aromas such as vanilla, along with the overpowering scent of flowers, "like in funeral home" will spontaneously and inexplicably engulf portions of the building.[5] David further recounted that "some of the craziest stories" include a woman's voice calling "Hello" from the kitchen when he was alone in the restaurant. Or the sound of what seems like a monstrous bowling ball heard crashing along the upstairs balcony. One evening when David was cleaning up with a barback and two other support staff after hours, he saw "something, maybe a shadow" moving toward the restroom. Certain that a customer remained inside the restaurant after closing, he summoned the other workers, and together they entered the washroom. All of them were unnerved to discover the bathroom was empty.

Another time, David was definitely alone in the building when he heard the trash can in the men's room being dragged across the floor. Checking on the noise, he found no one inside the room. Flummoxed, he turned and proceeded up the stairs to the balcony when the bathroom door mysteriously swung open on its own accord and then spontaneously slammed behind him. The frightened waiter didn't need any further prodding—he fled through the restaurant's front doors, severely bashing his shin in the process. In fact, Dave was so spooked that night that he didn't even pause to set the building's alarm system.[6]

A series of articles appearing in the *New Haven Register* during early 2019 inventoried an impressive assortment of ghostly disturbances. The list includes "flickering lights, a plume of smoke wafting across a room, a shadowy figure of a child and furniture moved by invisible hands from one place to another."[7]

The frightening appearance of a ghost child is a regular part of the restaurant's otherworldly activity: in Amy Bruni's supernatural cookbook *Food to Die For*, she shares the story of how a family abruptly departed the restaurant "because their four-year-old daughter was inconsolable, saying the girl at the next table was bothering her. There was no one at the table."[8]

Clairvoyant and tarot card reader Liliana Feliciano began working as a server at the Twisted Vine in late March 2024. She immediately sensed the

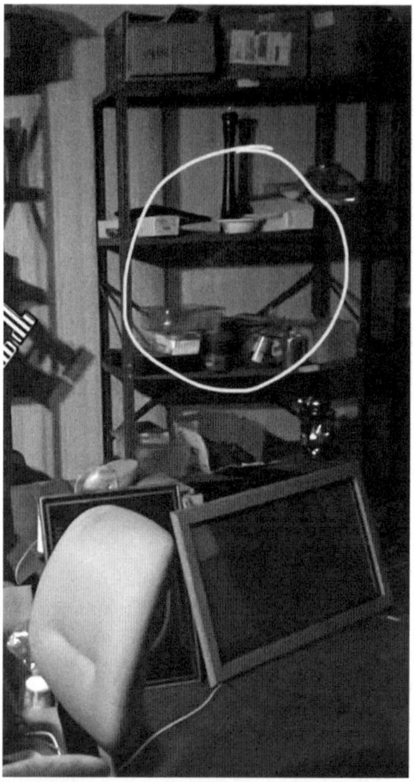

Left: Smoke Ghost. This photo, taken by clairvoyant Liliana Feliciano, shows a wispy plume of what appears to be fog materializing in the Twisted Vine Restaurant's second floor office. Though difficult to judge from this photo, a swirling mist is taking shape in the center of the room, in front of the shelf holding the tall pepper grinder. *Courtesy of Liliana Feliciano.*

Below: Two Things That Don't Go Well Together: Attics and Dolls. Toys are eerily arranged in the Twisted Vine Restaurant's attic. Psychics feel that these objects are helpful aids when attempting to contact the spirits of departed children. *Photograph by Michael J. Bielawa, taken April 11, 2024.*

volatile paranormal situation in the restaurant when, while looking out of the third-floor window facing Main Street, she saw the silhouettes of two male shadow figures reflected in the glass. There was nobody physically standing behind her.

Regarding the presence of youthful apparitions, the well-versed psychic-medium explained, "There are definitely ghost children here."[9] Liliana noted that she is aware of at least two spirit-children, "one girl and a boy, and they might be siblings." Remarkably, Feliciano has interacted with the ghost of the little girl that is so often witnessed by the restaurant's customers and staff. One of the most vivid spirit encounters Liliana experienced took place on Mother's Day 2024. Downstairs, while making an ice run, Feliciano said she felt "a breeze and saw a shadow run quickly" into the darkness of another room. She related that "it was a silhouette of a small child." On another occasion, after a ghost tour that featured a number of spiritualists, Liliana explained that the restaurant's spirits felt annoyed by the invasive psychics' prodding. Later, while inside one of the brick-arched rooms of the restaurant's lower level, she inquired aloud if the building's energy was calmed. At that instant, Liliana said she felt someone invisibly take her hand and that it was "definitely the hand of a little girl." As further proof illustrating the presence of children, Liliana noted that toys will appear and move around the same room where her hand was grasped. The spirit-child continues to connect with Feliciano, often playfully pinching her and tugging on Lily's belt.

But it is not all fun and games. Liliana, who carries on her family's tradition of psychic healing, cautions about the restaurant's attic ghosts: "There are certain dark corners there where Spirits abide. And they want to be left alone."

Based on Michael Picone's research, Feliciano subscribes to the legend that a house standing on this site, prior to the bank's construction, burned to the ground with the loss of two small children. In fact, during a recent séance held inside the restaurant (the Twisted Vine hosts an ongoing assortment of enthralling metaphysical events), the medium announced, without any prior knowledge of the restaurant's history, that "a man had set fire to a house on the site."[10]

THE SADDEST OF ALL HAUNTINGS

Individuals and paranormal organizations familiar with the Birmingham National Bank building's strange history continue to investigate and ponder a possible explanation for these perplexing experiences. Interestingly, one would think that the legends surrounding the bank's having served as a morgue or the grounds having been the scene of a deadly house fire would provide rational enough to explain the hauntings. However, most investigators point to a different, and far more powerful, presence: the ghost of Samuel Lessey.

Samuel H. Lessey (1858–1913) was a respectable, dedicated and hardworking pillar of the community. He may not have been as adventurous as his brother, Luther, the Derby dentist who departed for Seattle and then trekked farther north into the Klondike's gold fields. But Sam found his treasure locally, especially in helping others. He was involved in town politics, was active as a board member for the YMCA and served as president of the Birmingham Cemetery Association. Indeed,

Gate at Oak Cliff Cemetery. Samuel Lessey devoted his life to creating a beautiful burial ground for citizens of Derby, Connecticut. Now he too rests here. *Photograph by Michael J. Bielawa, August 11, 2024.*

View of Counting Station in 1896. Samuel Lessey worked for more than two decades at the Birmingham National Bank. *From C.B. Gillespie,* Souvenir History of Derby and Shelton, Connecticut. *The Transcript Company, 1896.*

it was under Lessey's guidance in 1897 that the graveyard on Hawthorne Avenue adopted the enduring name of Oak Cliff Cemetery.

Samuel was a steadfast employee for the Birmingham National Bank, where he worked day in and day out for a quarter of a century. Lessey elevated his situation from messenger boy to teller and then to assistant cashier; he was eventually promoted in June 1913 to the important position of bank cashier. But the new job provided Sam with an overabundance of stress. People noted that, "being anxious to 'make good,' he worked many hours overtime. His health [was not] as robust as usual the last few weeks, and his family [had] feared for some time that he would suffer a complete breakdown."[11] Samuel's friends witnessed a dark demeanor arrive along with the head cashier title: "the responsibilities of the position, which he had labored hard to fill, had unnerved him."[12]

Another big part of Samuel's worries derived from a loan his predecessor had advanced to the Derby Fur Fabric Company. Sam's opposition to this transaction proved prescient, since the textile company went bankrupt shortly thereafter, leaving the bank in a financial hole. And though he was in no way responsible for this ill-fated loan decision, Sam agonized over the negative effect it placed on his employer. Samuel Lessey did not need the freight of any additional worries—but that problem did manifest the day Earl Sherwood Steeves jauntily breezed through the Birmingham National Bank's ornate doors.

Earl Steeves was the son of a prominent Derby entrepreneur-grocer. The twenty-one-year-old followed the family tradition, and he became a "dealer in staple and fancy groceries."[13] Earl, however, became better known as a ne'er-do-well and conniving businessman. On the prowl for a quick buck, Steeves plotted an illegal check-cashing scheme. No gun, no bomb, no victims (or so Earl thought)—all that was required would be a signature and a dollar sign with a few added zeroes. Acquiring two bank checks made out to him by a Mrs. Mary A. Lavelle in the amounts of $10 and $15 each, Earl altered the dollar amounts to $1,000 and $1,500, respectively. This ploy was known as "check raising" (falsely increasing or raising a check's dollar amount). The thief cashed the checks and deposited them in the Birmingham National Bank. Earl then promptly transferred the money to an Ansonia bank, where he would withdraw the cash under an assumed name. Ever the efficient and helpful banker, Samuel Lessey smiled as he unwittingly completed Steeves's illegal transactions.

Soon afterward, as a result of the Seymour Trust Company inquiring into recent felonious behavior conducted by Steeves (Earl had deposited a check under a false name at Seymour Trust that he had raised from $25 to $2,500), the Birmingham National Bank, began its own internal inspection, which uncovered Earl's illegal activity in Derby. Samuel Lessey was approached by his supervisors. They berated the poor man—how could a longtime bank employee as well as a court-recognized handwriting authority[14] have been duped into cashing fake checks? The administrators were appalled. "Yes, yes, this calls for a full investigation. Absolutely! At the very least, Mr. Lessey, your oversight will be entered into your permanent record." A tallying of the bank's accounts would immediately commence, and the ledgers would be examined—with Mr. Lessey at the heart of the investigation!

Charles Nettleton, President of the Birmingham National Bank. A robbery blamed on Samuel Lessey by the bank's administration supposedly pushed the cashier to his utmost emotional limits. *From C.B. Gillespie,* Souvenir History of Derby and Shelton, Connecticut. *The Transcript Company, 1896.*

This was all too much for Sam. Imagine, after all these years of spotless service and now accused of working with a check-forger and of doctoring the bank's financial ledgers! But wait a moment, with the books opened, would Sam be exposed for misappropriating, or pocketing, funds sometime in the past?

The following Monday, November 17, 1913, Sam bid his wife goodbye a little before nine o'clock in the morning and left for work. He seemed buoyed by having attended the weekend's Yale-Princeton football game in New Haven with his son, Yale engineering student Samuel Kenric Lessey (after the contest, both Sams merely shrugged off the score, the game having ended in a 3–3 tie).

But Samuel H. Lessey never arrived at the bank.

After an hour or so, when it became apparent that Samuel wasn't going to report to work, his bosses contacted Sam's wife, Jennie. Mrs. Lessey retraced her husband's regular morning route. Sam was nowhere to be found. The last time he had been seen, Samuel was waiting at the trolley stop. Odd. Now the police needed to get involved. The authorities searched the city and sent bulletins to neighboring towns asking them to be on the lookout for Samuel Lessey. It was nearly twelve hours later that the first clue was discovered. Having exhausted all of the possible places where Sam might have sequestered himself, the search finally brought the police to Oak Cliff Cemetery.

As president of the cemetery association, Samuel had access to the grounds and buildings. Maybe his quest for a lonely and meditative location brought him to the bucolic knolls on the edge of town. It was past midnight when Chief of Police Daniel T. Odell, spotted Sam's coat draped at the entrance of the cemetery's public receiving vault. Pushing the heavy door open wide and entering the crypt, the chief along with Officer Kennedy were shocked at the gruesome sight they encountered: Sam's outstretched body lay in an open coffin box (this is the larger vessel that usually contains the casket), the banker's right hand still gripping a pistol. Samuel had climbed into the container, where he placed the revolver in his mouth and fired, the bullet lodging in his temple. Sam would never leave Oak Cliff Cemetery. He'd exchanged one vault at the bank for another vault here at the burial grounds. A rumor started that Sam's suicide was the result of his impending arrest due to the bank's newly launched investigation. Would discrepancies appear in Lessey's ledgers?

The following day, bank president Charles P. Nettleton declared that all of Lessey's accounts were "absolutely correct." Further speculation had the public attributing Sam's desperate act to the blame and censure assigned to him by Birmingham National Bank officials. The bank's administrators disavowed there being any connection.

Say a Prayer for Samuel Lessey. Oak Cliff Cemetery is often visited by those aware of the banker's sad and untimely demise. *Photograph by Michael J. Bielawa, taken August 11, 2024.*

If, indeed, the paranormal experiences taking place in the former bank building are due to innocent Sam Lessey choosing to end his life because of an unfounded scandal, then this would truly be the saddest of all hauntings.

Another Banker. Another Suicide? Another Ghost?

Something about the old bank seemed to summon desperate and dark emotions. Successful sixty-year-old businessman Rufus W. Blake stood atop the Naugatuck Valley's industrial world. He was the millionaire owner of two piano manufactories, Derby's world-renowned Sterling Piano Company and the Huntington Piano Company in Shelton. One of Blake's community-business responsibilities had him serving as a director for the Birmingham National Bank. The bank. Again. Even more exhilarating than Blake's business acumen was the man's marriage after merely a few weeks' romance to the stunning twenty-four-year-old Edith Mock. His first wife, Hannah, was just buried in 1899, and less than a year later, in 1900, he's marrying Miss Mock! Oh, how the town gossips smirked. No one really even knew the new Mrs. Blake; she was so aloof. Oh my, the audacity.[15]

Yet Rufus Blake was not happy with his lot in life. Lately, those close to the Derby manufacturer noted a pronounced melancholy gripping this captain of industry. Then, on the night of October 17, 1901, after playing cards with his wife in their drawing room, Blake slowly walked up the stairs of their Elizabeth Street mansion in Derby. Entering Philipp Mock's dressing room (Philipp, Edith's brother, was living with the couple), Blake removed a prized pistol from his brother-in-law's gun collection. The weapon either discharged by accident or on purpose (depending on which newspaper coverage one subscribed to). "The bullet entered just below [Mr. Blake's] right eye, passed back of the nose, and, carrying some of the eye with it, emerged through the left optic cavity."[16] Blake passed away nine days later. No one ever ascertained how the revolver's metal barrel came

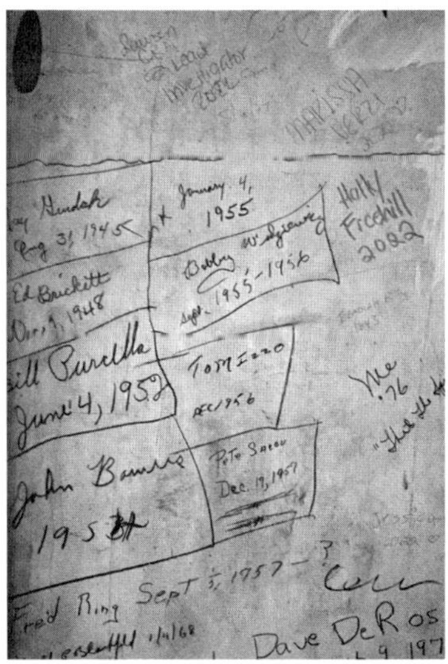

Left: Bank Director Rufus Blake's May-December Downfall. The Birmingham National Bank holds a legacy of unfounded scandal and definite suicide. Note: weirdly, this photo thwarted repeated attempts to be scanned for inclusion in this book. *From C.B. Gillespie,* Souvenir History of Derby and Shelton, Connecticut. *The Transcript Company, 1896.*

Right: Endorse Here, Please. A long-standing tradition at the Birmingham National Bank had employees write their names on the bank's attic wall. How many of these tellers might have witnessed something supernatural? *Photograph by Michael J. Bielawa.*

to be pointed at Blake's face—or, for that matter, if the decision to end his life, if it was suicide, had anything to do with Blake's possible insecurity about having a beautiful young wife. Was there some kind of financial trouble at his factories, or was there something amiss at the Birmingham Bank: no one knew.

No one, that is, unless he confessed to Sam Lessey once the ever-helpful bank cashier joined him in the afterlife at Oak Cliff Cemetery.[17]

PART II
GENII LOCORUM

7

Inside the Naugatuck Valley Vortex

Strange Sights Overhead

I bring you a warning: Every one of you listening to my voice, tell the world, tell this to everybody wherever they are. Watch the skies. Everywhere. Keep looking. Keep watching the skies.
—closing line from the 1951 film The Thing from Another World

The dark skies above Waterbury are no stranger to the mysterious. Tantalizing, and at times frightening, "things" have been observed flying over the Naugatuck Valley. During the course of the past 150 years, there has been a glut of perplexing eyewitness accounts regarding unexplainable sightings: sky cylinders, glowing triangles, inexplicable lights, balls of flame and the pervasive mid-century "flying saucer" have all made appearances here as if leaping from a golden age sci-fi movie screen. Though descriptions of these objects may vary, one constant remains: the valley has long been observed by an enigmatic aerial presence that continues to monitor the entire length of the Naugatuck River. This UFO hot spot is the Naugatuck Valley Vortex.

Indeed, shocking unidentified aerial/anomalous phenomena (UAP) and otherworldly events have occurred within the entire southwestern fringe of New England. This region, including the area where Connecticut's border meets with neighboring Massachusetts and New York, has provided fodder for some of the world's most infamous alien encounters. The spectrum of events include: visitations by the Men in

Black at Albert Bender's home in Bridgeport, Connecticut; the Thom Reed incidents in Sheffield, Massachusetts; the Pine Bush Phenomenon in New York; and of course, the pervasive UAP observations occurring within the Hudson Valley Triangle.

Dr. J. Allen Hynek, the civilian scientific advisor for the U.S. Air Force's seventeen-year-long UFO study, Project Bluebook, writes of this phenomenon. He notes in his work, *Night Siege: The Hudson Valley UFO Sightings*, that "[UFO] sightings [have] occurred over a 1,400-square mile area covering Westchester, Putnam, and Dutchess Counties in New York, and neighboring Fairfield, Litchfield and New Haven Counties in Connecticut."[1]

Here is a selection of some of the earliest, and certainly most eerie, examples of UAP encounters occurring in and adjacent to the Naugatuck Valley Vortex:

CASE I

City: Winchester, Connecticut
Locale: Highland Lake
Date: Saturday, August 4, 1888

Something profoundly strange took place high above western Connecticut during a Saturday afternoon in the month of August 1888. What appeared to be an approaching summer shower quickly morphed into an alarming maelstrom. Compelling factors associated with this weather event lend themselves to a possible connection with an otherworldly occurrence here in the lonely hills of northwestern Connecticut.

That singular day would be long remembered. During the early afternoon, witnesses became aware of the cloudy horizon abruptly turning Bible-black. The gloomy mass began swirling, ever swifter, in the direction of a focal point known only to these dismal clouds and the Devil. Scattered across the region, city dwellers and farmers alike lifted amazed eyes to watch this emerging cloud storm churn toward a singular central point in the sky. Suddenly, an incredible fury was unleashed from on high. It seemed as if church bells tolling the three o'clock hour had summoned the severe rain, devastating winds and especially the unearthly incident that was soon to follow. Terrifying lightning strikes blanketed the state. Trees, barns, homes and every tall structure in the path of the monster storm were in imminent danger of being shattered by the jagged bolts thundering down from the black clouds. A Winsted barn located on North Main Street, near Smith Hill, was struck by lightning and burned to the ground. A barn in West Hartland and two more barns in Simsbury were hit by lightning. The electrical ribbons marched eastward with the storm in what seemed like some bounding shapeless colossus on stilts. "Inhabitants," in East Granby, "beheld the novel spectacle of a burning green tree."[2] The towering chestnut measured sixteen feet in circumference at its base and was "in full leaf and bearing a heavy crop of nuts." Despite its wet, verdant foliage, the tree was set ablaze by one of this storm's hellish bolts. Flames from the exploding tree shot fifty feet skyward while the eviscerated trunk was reduced to charcoal. Lightning killed four cows in Southbury; in the same village, another bolt splintered a huge elm tree.[3] Moving eastward, at four o'clock, a home in Waterbury's Buck's Hill neighborhood was invaded by the storm's fluid electricity. "The bolt entered at the chimney and then scattered in several directions…before escaping through the stovepipe hole."[4] In Hartford, cattle were killed, and of special note, the city's telegraph wires were "disturbed." Farther southeast in a wide area around New Haven, "telephone and telegraph wires and electric lights were seriously affected."

But by far, the most extraordinary episode associated with the strange cloud formation and its blistering lightning was the report of a massive projectile seen careening out from the black sky and crashing into Winsted's Highland Lake. Make no mistake, something very large and extremely powerful, described as a "ball of fire," rumbled into this lake on that August afternoon.[5] Known as Long Lake at the time, this body of water stretches three miles within the small town of Winchester in Connecticut's northwest corner. Residents living along the banks of Long Lake at the time explained that they were blinded by a "vivid flash of lightning, followed by a terrific peel [*sic*] of thunder." Then, following a "great roar," the awed spectators saw a "huge flame" fall from the sky. This ball of fire was said to be at least ten feet in length and was heading straight for Long Lake. When the burning object hit the water's surface, it generated huge waves. Acting like a "gigantic plow," the thing generated billows rising twenty feet high on each side of the furrow it created, all the while speeding pretty much the entire length of the lake.[6] Finally, when it was 100 yards from reaching the shore, there was another great crash of lightning, whereupon the fiery body quickly sank. Over the shattered and charred remains of that dreadful day, and well into the terrifying night, residents kept vigil on Long Lake. Watching. What was

Early Twentieth-Century View of Highland/Long Lake in Winsted. An extraterrestrial object fell into this lake one summer day. The impact parted the water in a huge and fiery trough. *Author's collection.*

it that fell from the sky on August 4, 1888? Whatever the unknown object might have been, locals were wary to note, "It was many hours before the waters of the lake became calm."

Waterbury, the largest city within the Naugatuck Valley Vortex, has had its own exhaustive share of UAP sightings. Here are some early and astonishing encounters:

CASE II

City: Waterbury, Connecticut
Locale: Buck's Hill
Date: Various nights, July–August 1892

Summer evenings provide the perfect time for a stroll. A casual walk through the park and around the neighborhood brings a nod to passing neighbors and the opportunity to catch a cool breeze. But Brass City residents felt compelled to leave their homes and gaze skyward for a much different reason during the summer of 1892. As July concluded that year, and particularly as August began in 1892, people were heading for Waterbury's open air in order to catch a glimpse of what was termed, in contemporary language, a "mysterious fire balloon." Any mention of a large balloon in those days would quickly call to mind county-fair aeronauts ascending skyward in a wicker gondola-type basket suspended below the craft's glowing flame. However, in these 1892 Waterbury incidents, no balloon or other lighter-than-air vehicle was ever observed. The glowing object was seen by a multitude of citizens. Curiously, the object witnessed may not have been a balloon. The author of a contemporary letter to the editor, signed only "Star Gazer," postulated that the witnesses of the nocturnal UAP may have confused the glowing object with the planet Mars, and that the bright light was "only a star after all."[7] Noting the implausibility of this argument, the *Waterbury Daily American* wrote that the object "came from the western horizon about 9:30 [at night], [and] sailed up to the meridian and away to the east, crossing the path of Mars."[8]

CASE III

City: Waterbury, Connecticut
Locale: Southeast of downtown, Scovill Manufacturing Company
Date: March 9–10, 1916

While French and German infantry valiantly clambered from their mud choked trenches to race back and forth across no-man's-land during the bloody Battle of Verdun, far across the Atlantic, workers at a sprawling New England munitions factory found themselves confronting their own unique battle. A battle whose weaponry was very different from those employed by Europe's warring nations. The weapon these Connecticut mill hands would soon come face to face with were not bullets or artillery shells or even poison gas but rather an armament aimed at destroying their sanity. These Waterbury workers had no idea that they were about to cross into their own bizarre battleground of an otherworldly kind: a no-man's-land expressly manufactured for the Naugatuck Valley Vortex.

It was the "thing," that menacing "thing" seen hovering overhead in the late-night sky; the otherworldly thing that would soon be termed, with a shudder of disbelief, the "big black object"[9] that drove Waterbury into madness. Whatever this large mystifying airborne body might have been, it remained stationary above the Scovill Manufactory Company's vast complex, casting a supremely bright beam of light earthward. Fanning ever slowly left and right (between East Main Street and old Bridge Street), this ray bleached the mill's array of red brick and black-sooty buildings into a pool of monochrome neon silver. Mesmerized by what was taking

WATERBURY REPUBLICAN

WHOLE NUMBER 10,129 FOURTEEN PAGES WATERBURY, CONN., FRIDAY, MARCH 10, 1916. FOURTEEN PAGES TWO CENTS

MYSTERIOUS AIRCRAFT VISITS SCOVILL'S; U.S. SOLDIERS CROSS BORDER INTO MEXICO

TROOPERS CHASE VILLA BANDITS WHO KILL AMERICANS CITIZENS OVER LINE---MEXICAN LOSS 100

Raiders Creep Upon New Mexico City at Early Dawn, While Residents Are Sleeping, and, Shouting "Death to Americans," Begin Bombardment. Civilians Fire on Attacking Force From Windows and Troops Drive Them Out—Casualties Light—Woman Tells Story of Capture by Villa's Men—Her Babe Given to Mexican Family—Senator Would Raise Army of 500,000 for Intervention—Machine Guns Fail to Work.

MACHINE GUNS FAILED TO WORK

El Paso, Tex., March 9—Failure of the machine guns to work in the fight between the Villa bandits and the Thirteenth cavalry at Columbus was responsible for the escape of the Villa bandits across the border and for the small loss of life among them, according to Private Thomas Barton of the hospital corps.

Washington, March 9.—Washington stands squarely behind Gen. Slocum in sending his cavalrymen into Mexico in pursuit of Francisco Villa and his band of outlaws who raided Columbus, N. M., today, murdering American soldiers and citizens and firing the town.

Secretary Lansing tonight informed the de facto government of Mexico thru Eliso Arredondo, its ambassador here, that he trusted no objection would be made to the action of the American troops, they having followed what is known in military circles as a "hot trail." No orders have been issued for the [illegible]

already had crossed. Later Mr. Arredondo called upon Sec. Lansing, express regret for the Villa raid, and was informed of the attitude of the United States.

Mr. Arredondo said he would communicate with Gen. Carranza immediately.

In expressing a hope that the Carranza government would not object to the crossing of the troops, the state department was [illegible]

COMMANDER OF MEXICAN BANDITS

PROPOSES ARMY OF 500,000 MEN TO ENTER MEXICO

Senator Fall of New Mexico Prepares Resolution to Recruit Big Force.

TO HELP AUTHORITIES STAMP OUT BRIGANDAGE

APPEARS ABOVE PLANT NEAR MIDNIGHT; GUARDS THROWN INTO TURMOIL

Brilliant Searchlight is Turned on Factory—Watchmen and Special Police Watch in Open-Mouthed Amazement Strange Craft, W[illegible] Hovers Over Building and Disappears in [illegible] Police Refuse to Discuss Affair—Alarm G[illegible] by Watchman at Main Gate—New Danger [illegible] Manufacturers of Explosives Seen.

Flying high over the plant of the Scovill Mfg. Co., with its bulk outlined against the sky, and with a brilliant light trained [illegible] ward, a mysterious aircraft, seen by numerous persons abo[illegible] Scovill plant, created a sensation just before midnight last night [illegible] aircraft sailed peacefully to the eastward, with the bright light [illegible] ing visibly until it became a tiny speck in the distance.

Guards around the Scovill plant were thrown into a tu[illegible] When the aircraft was first discovered it seemed to be ho[illegible] directly above the Scovill factory. While the guards and wor[illegible] were standing open-mouthed, glancing skyward, the big shap[illegible] seen to move slowly and then more rapidly across the heavens, [illegible] disappearing.

GUARDS SEE AIRCRAFT

Several of the guards reported they had seen the aircraft, [illegible] trained its lights down on the factories in the Naugatuck valley [illegible] could not distinguish without glasses whether the prowling [illegible] was a balloon or a dirigible, or a heavier than air machine, o[illegible] monoplane type.

The first appearance of the aircraft indicated that it had co[illegible] from the westward over the large manufacturing plants of the [illegible] casting its bright lights downward, moving more slowly over [illegible] plants than when it had cleared the Scovill property to the eastw[illegible]

The watchman at the main gate of the Scovill plant was the [illegible] coverer of the mysterious craft. He immediately spread the al[illegible] and guards about the factory were informed of the aircraft hov[illegible] above. They could easily distinguish the light on the moving [illegible]

The Aliens Are Watching. This alarming front-page headline announced to the world that something strange was happening in the skies over the Naugatuck Valley. *From* Waterbury Republican, *March 10, 1916.*

Scovill Plant. Did visitors from beyond earth set their sights on this major American armament manufacturer? UFO/UAP sightings near nuclear power plants and sensitive military installations continue to occur around the world to this very day. *From T.M. Fowler and Hughes & Bailey. Aero view of Waterbury, Connecticut. Boston, Hughes & Fowler, 1917. Map. https://www.loc.gov/item/gm71005376/.*

place overhead, witnesses would later remark how hundreds of hardboiled laborers and factory guards "watched [in] open-mouthed amazement [as the] strange craft" hovered over the plant.[10]

The first to lay widening eyes on the "big black object" was Arthur Daniels, a watchman at Scovill's main gate. The time was just a little before midnight (the day turning into Friday, March 10) when Daniels's attention was called skyward. Unable to comprehend exactly what this immense object might be and, more importantly, the reason for its looming presence, the guard instinctively sounded the plant's alarm bells. The clanging summons brought the factory's small security army rushing from their stations toward the front gate. Assembling beneath the large craft outlined against the night sky threw the Scovill guards into, what the front page of the *Waterbury Republican* would bellow from its headline that day, a state of complete "turmoil."[11]

The ensuing cacophony of jarring bells and workers' shouts woke the crowded neighborhood surrounding Scovill's. This initial commotion cascaded street by street throughout the city. Panic "spread rapidly"[12] as "thousands of people" leaped from their beds[13] to catch an eye-popping glimpse of "the big black object" slowly maneuvering eastward away from the factory.

For anyone claiming that these events may have been a mass hallucination or an elaborately conceived newspaper hoax, Reverend Edward J. Brennan of Waterbury's St. Margaret's Church came forward to attest about his own experience. The forty-eight-year-old former U.S. Navy chaplain (Brennan served in the navy from 1901 to 1909) explained that while he was riding the trolley that night, along with a number of other passengers, they all saw "a low light moving slowly" in the sky. The priest related how "the light followed the route of the car." Everyone aboard the trolley watched the object with enthralled amazement until its view became obscured by trees.[14]

Among the hundreds of people at Scovill's, none of those witnessing the strange event were able to "distinguish whether the prowling craft was a balloon, or a dirigible, or a heavier-than-air machine of a monoplane type."[15] Gliding away in complete silence, the object suddenly "sped eastward"[16] until "it became a tiny speck in the distance."[17] Not only is the speed of the craft noteworthy, but an additional strange fact concerns the object's propulsion as well: the lack of any sound. During an era when aeroplanes and dirigibles were powered by loud motors, in no instance did witnesses describe the noise generated by propellers or familiar machines.

Attempting to mollify those of the opinion that the armaments plant had been endangered by some outside force, John H. Goss, superintendent of Scovill, pronounced that the big object was merely a toy balloon with a stream of lights attached.[18] When the craft shockingly visited Waterbury again the following night, any theory about the object being some sort of balloon was eliminated. Observers noted that the wind was blowing "from the westward…and the craft moved [against the wind] in a westward direction."[19]

No Higher Authority. "The light followed the route of the car," according to respected and popular reverend Edward J. Brennan. He was one of the many trolley passengers who witnessed an unidentified aerial object over Waterbury during the First World War. *William J. Pape, ed.* History of Waterbury and the Naugatuck Valley, Connecticut, *vol. 3, S.J. Clarke Publishing, 1918.*

Whatever this object may have been, and wherever it originated, the fact that the craft was monitoring an important World War I–era munitions factory mirrors UAP situations plaguing the world today: unidentified aerial phenomena are being reported currently in the proximity of technologically sensitive (and dangerous) areas such as atom bomb test sites, nuclear waste facilities, power plants and naval task forces.[20]

In yet another harbinger of things to come, when the UAP appeared over Scovill in 1916, the Waterbury police station was inundated with calls and visits from concerned citizens reporting the strange flying object. Local authorities could have never foretold that their reply on that remarkable March night would one day become a routine response known around the world to anyone reporting UFO activity: "The [Waterbury] police would not discuss the matter. When called, the desk lieutenant refused to affirm or deny [the event]."[21]

8

The Kinneytown Entity

Like one, that on a lonesome road
Doth walk in fear and dread,
And having once turned round walks on,
And turns no more his head;
Because he knows, a frightful fiend
Doth close behind him tread.
— Samuel Taylor Coleridge, The Rime of the Ancient Mariner, *1798*

"What? Do you think, then, that this thing is ——"
"I don't know what it is," was the solemn reply; "but please the gods
I will, with your assistance, thoroughly investigate it."
— Fitz-James O'Brien, "What Was It?" 1859

The road is very lonely on the Kinneytown flats.
*—*Ansonia Evening Sentinel, *September 8, 1897*

Folklore is replete with tales of haunted thoroughfares. Trace these disturbing geographical features on the roadmap of fear in the atlas of the supernatural. These cursed locales include lonely highways where spirit hitchhikers silently thumb their eternal homebound rides and dusty midnight crossroads where unholy contracts are signed in blood. Certain moonlit lanes will always be shunned. Such roads do exist. And they exist here in the Naugatuck Valley.

Few remember vibrant Kinneytown. Situated roughly two miles below downtown Seymour, this hardscrabble hamlet was sprawled along the west bank of the Naugatuck River's flats and highlands. The origin of the area's name can be found in the fascinating 1902 book *Seymour, Past and Present*; in these pages, several historians remark on how the early "Kenney" family spread northward up the Naugatuck Valley and eventually settled on the outskirts of Humphreysville. The first Kenney to settle at what would become Kinneytown was William, born in 1757, the ninth son of Welsh immigrant Ebenezer Kenney. At some point, the clan assumed the Gaelic "Kinney" spelling of their surname. The preponderance of homes here were inhabited by plain folk displaying a "Kenney" surname, which would eventually morph into "Kinney."

The river's flatlands here quickly rise into the rugged terrain where sparkling brooks tumble toward the Naugatuck, ripe for powering Kinney sawmills, cider mills and a ropeworks factory. The hamlet's birth and fall were meteoric. By 1900, all that lingered from the first Kenney/Kinney homestead were the stones lining a shallow cellar hole found along the river "under the shadow of a cherry tree."[1] Today, all that exists of the Kinneytown settlement are a few place names, such as the Kinneytown Dam, whose cascading waters once drove the downstream gears of Ansonia's factories. The original dam, built during the 1840s, was located immediately north of the current structure.

Wading into the opening decades of the twentieth century, Valley residents could easily point to the shadow of Kinneytown. Such inquiries

Kinneytown, 1921. (Seen here beneath the word "Seymour.") By the turn of the twentieth century all that remained of the isolated hamlet was a handful of scattered houses and the roads blending into the forested hills. *From Hughes & Bailey. Aero view of Ansonia, Connecticut. [Waterbury, Conn, 1921] Map. https://www.loc.gov/item/75693145/.*

were usually met with a curious gaze implying, "What do you want there?" Everybody knew something was amiss in Kinneytown. All you had to do was read the newspapers: sometimes reports would mention how a horse would inexplicably refuse to advance when approaching one of the mountain's winding roads but instead bolt off in a different direction. During the 1920s, an article noted a peculiar infestation of rats. On another occasion, a vast and hideous murder of crows descended on these banks and devastated the trees lining the shore. The river itself, near the dam, sadly experienced several drownings. By mid-century, traces of this village that the 1955 flood hadn't obliterated had already been forgotten. Except for the cartographer's italicized lettering that still delineates "Kinneytown Brook," the village doesn't seem to ever have existed. But the looming hills of olden Kinneytown continue to hold a certain unnatural feel.

The aforementioned *Seymour, Past and Present* cautiously notes one particularly eerie area: a "very old forsaken road…marked by a lane near the Kenny [*sic*] homestead…winding up the hill westward, meeting the Bungay road."[2] An 1868 map of the Town of Seymour illustrates the most likely spot that these historians were discussing was a trail leading away from the river, past a sawmill and fading into the woods. If whispers are to be trusted and shadows believed, this was the entrance to the realm of the Kinneytown "Entity."

At the close of the nineteenth century, a series of unexplained events gripped this part of the Naugatuck Valley. "All Kinneytown" was cast into a "state of fear" according to the November 18, 1896 *Ansonia Evening Sentinel*.[3] Witnesses refused to discuss in detail or offered only incoherent statements when asked about an ongoing haunting taking place along a certain seldom used stretch of a Kinneytown road. Individuals traveling these dark hills attested that the Entity could not be seen with their eyes, but rather, when anyone happened to be unlucky enough to venture near the supernatural presence, they physically sensed an enveloping evil. The *New York Sun* on November 29, 1896,[4] explained that the Entity "manifests itself in the phantasm of an invisible hand." Quite interestingly, this peculiar feature of the Kinneytown Entity correlates with worldwide paranormal phenomena concerning haunted roads.[5]

The *New York Sun* article continues that the invisible creature was usually encountered "stretching forth its grisly hand from a roadside thicket and barring the road to a woodsman's oxen or horses, as the Kinneytown ghost has been doing…no one knows just what it is." The unnamed New York reporter proffered an unnerving observation: "At any rate, it is not a shape or form; it is a presence."[6]

Word came down out of the Kinneytown woods that Peter Hinckley encountered something strange. Breathlessly he told the handful of men gathered around the apple barrels in the little Kinneytown grocery store that what he experienced happened "not long after nightfall." Hinckley explained that he was heading home, walking alone on the road above Kinneytown, "when a spectral hand, cold and benumbing, was laid on his chest and shoulder."[7] The startled man "felt his hair and hat uprising together." Reiterating what every witness unfortunate enough to meet the Entity would unwaveringly swear: Hinckley was utterly incapable of movement. Peter tried to run, he told the old graybeards around the store's counter, but no matter how much he strained and pulled, he felt paralyzed. Hinckley mimicked straining and grimaced to illustrate how "his feet [had] seemed glued to the roadbed." Over time, others would seek refuge at the Kinneytown grocery and step up onto the creaking porch, white-knuckling one of the store's posts looking pale and shaken. The old men inside would just look at each other and nod knowingly. If those frightened visitors had witnessed anything odd, they weren't saying what it was that they'd seen. Or felt.

That wasn't the case with Minott Smith. Minott was anxious to talk with newspaper reporters about what he experienced over in Kinneytown. When Smith decided to share his thoughts, locals saw him as a man to be taken seriously. The thirty-four-year-old was a nose-to-the-grindstone fellow not known for exaggeration. He'd been a farmer most of his life, having grown up on, and inheriting, his grandfather's sprawling acres nestled near Twomile Brook on the Derby-Orange town line.[8]

Minott somberly described his personal Kinneytown incident: it was the late autumn of 1896, and now heading back to his farm, Minott Smith opted for the most direct route through the Seymour hills. Business had occupied him longer than expected in the north country. Gnarled branches flexed and hissed in the breeze above Smith's wagon as it grumbled along the rutted Kinneytown Road. Minott peered into the night; the swaying shadows made the woods seem deeper. And darker. He snapped the reins of his horse to quicken the animal's pace. Maybe it was a coincidence, but Minott Smith's run-in with whatever "it" was took place around the same time as a meteor shower illuminated Seymour's sky.

The *Waterbury Democrat* on November 18, 1896, reported that Minott A. Smith "has seen it, and it gave him an experience which he says he does not care to have repeated."[9] The *New York Sun* of November 29, 1896, detailed Smith's encounter:

> *In the darkest and loneliest outlying district…he discerned the outlines of a spectral image imprinted on the solid-seeming midnight blackness….* [Minott Smith] *concluded that the presence was palpable rather than visible. He had felt it. It seemed to loom right ahead of him, above his steed….The farmer commanded his horse with a sharp yell and fitfully shook the reins, but the Entity "shot downward* [with] *malevolent intent, and seized his horse's tail with both its diabolical hands and shook and twisted with ghoulish glee." The horse and carriage seemed frozen, rooted in their tracks, "Again, Minott fancied that he distinguished the outlines of a looming figure and that he heard laughter, shrill and chuckling, but elusive and void, like an outcry heard in a dream." The terrified horse struggled but remained fastened to the dirt lane. Upon finally being released from the Entity's clutches, Smith and his horse raced uphill with the invisible presence shrieking closely behind the wagon's tailboard. When questioned, Smith recounted how during the first few seconds of their escape he had "no doubt the Kinneytown ghost or specter was perched on the horse's crupper* [a leather loop running under the tail and up to the saddle], *prying or wrenching at the tail."*[10]

Another strange incident took place during November 1896: very late one night, a group of bicyclists confronted a weird sight next to the Naugatuck River on the Kinneytown Flats. Enjoying a midnight trek out of Ansonia, the wheelmen spontaneously came to a skidding halt. Down the road near the Roswell Kinney place, an ominous figure emerged from the thick brush. Squinting into the gloom, the cyclists attempted to make sense of the swaying image before them. Someone, or *something*, was draped entirely in white. Maybe, they thought, it was a toga. As if that weren't bizarre enough, the unearthly wanderer was playing a rustic hornpipe.[11] Odd music, shrill and primitive, filled the loathsome road. A Seymour newspaper dismissed the entire episode as a teenage prank. But the cloaked form was seen on two other occasions. Folks up and down the hills of Kinneytown wondered if the dancing shape in pale robes was attempting to honor the great god Pan or whether this was a way to appease, or maybe exorcise, the Entity of the woods.

Did an invisible presence once roam a hamlet in the Naugatuck Valley? One has to wonder if the Kinneytown Entity is still out there, watching. Deep

The Road to Madness. One of Kinneytown's seldom used and caliginous backroads was featured in this circa 1900 photograph. *Author's collection.*

in the woods. On a desolate stretch of road. Lurking inside the brush and brambles just beyond the pale headlights' radius, looming within the reach of passing cars. Should, by any chance, you find yourself in long forgotten Kinneytown and your vehicle suddenly stalls, perhaps it's better to lock the doors…and wait for the screeching laughter to pass.

WALKING DISTANCE: ESCAPING THE KINNEYTOWN ENTITY

The majority of eyewitness accounts state that the Kinneytown Entity wanders the hills and riverbank of the Bungay woods. An obvious, and unnerving, question arises when one considers the possible extent in which the Entity might be able to travel: Did, or could, the Entity leave the forested highlands and venture into downtown Seymour? Though most recorded manifestations have occurred within Kinneytown proper, on at least one occasion, the Entity materialized on the outskirts of Seymour's business district. Victims reported an unidentified "thing" lurking on the west bank of the Naugatuck, near the Broad Street Bridge.

Perhaps the most striking downtown confrontation occurred during 1901, when a pair of local men experienced an uncanny visitation while returning to their homes late one November

Power Over Evil. A demonic creature burst forth from a wooded area across the street from the Seymour Congregational Church in 1901. Did this holy edifice divert the monster's path away from downtown? This is how the church would have looked at the time of the reported incident. *Author's collection.*

night. It was an encounter they would not, for any amount of money, wish to repeat.[12] After leaving Seymour's commercial center, the two shared a portion of their walk; one of the gentlemen resided on Derby Avenue, and the other was heading back to Bungay Hill. Chuckling over their evening's escapades, their conversation abruptly halted as they exited the Broad Street Bridge. Sounds of a commotion emanating from the nearby woods froze them in place. Something very large was thrashing through the thicket across from the Congregational church. What they later reported to the authorities was bizarre: a creature crashed out of the trees and charged after them with a soul-shattering cry. The men immediately fled, both running in different directions. Taking a wide and roundabout route back toward Kinneytown, they eventually arrived breathlessly at their respective homes. Before having raced off, however, they had a moment to observe the Entity. These men provided identical descriptions of the hideous creature. The being, they explained, had green eyes and long horns sprouting from its head. As described in other surreal Kinneytown sightings, its body was draped in white. Perhaps most disturbing of all, the men stated that the thing stood ten feet tall. Multiple reports were made by individuals during that autumn of 1901 claiming to have seen some sort of creature, or ghost, in the same locale.

What summoned the creature down off the hillside? Might the fact that these two men both lived in the area haunted by the Kinneytown Entity have anything to do with their being stalked by the horned beast? Was there a reason why this creature was seen lurking only on the western side of the Broad Street Bridge? Did the sanctity of the adjacent church halt the monster's attack? There may be another reason why the Entity does not venture into downtown Seymour: some folklorists suggest that unclean spirits, vampires and witches are unable to cross water since it is a purifying element.[13] But there is always the question of whether the Entity's wandering ways might bring it back to the outskirts of downtown again.[14]

9

Seymour's Empty Sepulcher Sings a Silent Chantey

Secrets are often interred within the consecrated soil of New England graveyards. One family plot in particular, near the crest of Seymour, Connecticut's Great Hill Cemetery, lends itself to a bizarre legacy. Far removed from any ocean breeze, a nautical mystery lays firmly anchored in this landlocked Naugatuck Valley boneyard. This is the grave of father and son Ephraim and Joseph Wooster, two Great Hill Ishmaels who encountered fate's awful waves. Neither Derby, Connecticut man's earthly remains are buried beneath their chiseled names. Instead, the ground here has been cursed with terror-filled tides in this final resting place of horror.

Only the jagged lower portion of the gravestone lingers; the age-stained marker's top half, bearing the name of Ephraim Wooster, has long since vanished. Who, or what, found satisfaction in eliminating Ephraim's name from this hillside? Identifying the site as belonging to Ephraim can be determined through cemetery records associated with his son's name, Joseph Wooster, which is chiseled on the bottom of the stone.[1] However, the true macabre mystery is created thereupon by these two faded sentences:

…who was killed by the
explosion of a steam boat
boiler Sept. 11, 1830 and
buried in New York, aged 66
Also his son

JOSEPH D. WOOSTER
died at New Iberia Jan. 26
1832, and buried on the
Island of Belize aged 31.

Every few years, a lone passerby on this hillside might, pause to trace with anxious fingertips the Woosters' obliterated epitaph and wonder what happened to these forgotten men? For generations, this grave marker has remained Seymour's sphinx. Until now.

THE STORY OF EPHRAIM

Ephraim Wooster was in lower Manhattan drowning under a sea of paperwork. It was just three days prior to the Derby man's sixty-sixth birthday, and he wanted to get back home to Connecticut. Ephraim decided to leave

A Landlocked Cemetery's Nautical Legacy. The Wooster family's blasted gravestone, actually a cenotaph, is located near the crest of Great Hill Cemetery in Seymour, Connecticut. What remains of the obliterated engraving holds a tragic tale. *Photograph by Michael J. Bielawa, taken February 3, 2023.*

work early, so corking his ink bottle and slamming shut the leather cover of an oversized ledger, he sauntered off in the direction of the East River. Diving into a vest pocket, he confirmed his boat ticket with a reassuring squeeze. Proceeding down Maiden Lane, Ephraim silently regarded how much Manhattan had grown since the War for Independence. Victory over the king had taken place only half a century earlier. Unbelievably, it was now 1830, and by Jove, Ephraim's world had changed so splendidly. "Progress is seen everywhere," he marveled, "railroad tracks being laid in Harlem and steamboats clanging all along the bustling waterfront." Once upon a time, he was "Sargent Wooster" of the Connecticut militia,[2] but now old warrior Wooster was contented citizen-merchant Wooster of the Naugatuck Valley on one of his regular business jaunts to America's largest metropolis.

Impelled by his bracing stroll and the city's verve, Ephraim contemplated his own life's journey. Over the course of his six-plus decades, the Waterbury-born man had held a variety of government positions, including school commissioner. At the commencement of the nineteenth century, Ephraim had served as tax collector for the state. Now a respected

History and Beauty and Sadly, Sometimes Misery. A stroll among Great Hill Cemetery's forlorn hillside invokes the voices of New England's romantic and eerie past. *Photograph by Michael J. Bielawa, taken September 9, 2024.*

merchant, he smiled happily, anticipating the short trip home to his wife, Mittie, in Derby, Connecticut.[3]

Reaching South Street, Ephraim witnessed boisterous stevedores and sailors from around the world. Crews cajoled in camaraderie on the cobblestone streets, others sang work songs high up in the rigging of coastal schooners and hidden voices ballyhooed deep within the hatches of large ocean clippers. It was the New Haven–bound steamship the *United States* Ephraim sought. This steamer's afternoon voyage departed in an hour, allowing Ephraim time to contemplate the dockside activity. Perched near the gangplank, the Derby entrepreneur reached into his pocket and removed his passage receipt. Studying the paper, he confirmed the day's date carefully inked on the stub. The concept of individual steamboat tickets was a novelty that Captain Beecher of the *United States* had himself instituted on these wharves.[4] "Not having to wait in a line or scramble for a fare certainly was more convenient," weighed Ephraim. Looking down at the voucher in his hand, Wooster noted the date: September 11. Yes, September 11, 1830.

Ephraim cast a measured glance, bow to stern, at the *United States*, moored in the swirling waters of the East River. The sturdy craft had been

Maiden Lane, Southern Manhattan. This is exactly what the scene looked like when, on September 11, 1830, Ephraim Wooster took his last earthbound steps along these docks. *New York Public Library Digital Collection.*

The Steamship *United States*. Constructed in 1821, the *United States* was among the earliest vessels to provide regular steam service between New Haven and New York City. A few years after its christening, disaster struck the ship at Hell's Gate passage. *From Samuel Ward Stanton,* American Steam Vessels. *Smith and Stanton, 1895.*

constructed in New York nine years earlier in 1821. It measured 140 feet in length and propelled itself with paddlewheels situated on both port and starboard sides. Initially, the *United States* carried passengers up and down the Hudson River, between Perth Amboy in New Jersey and Albany. Thereafter, it was briefly employed for trips between New York City and Newark.[5] The ship's fate would be dramatically altered the following year, in 1822, when she was purchased by the newly founded New Haven Steamboat Company.[6]

During these early steamboat days, nothing came easy for owners or passengers. The New York Legislature willfully created a monopoly on its own waters by granting steam rights to descendants of steamboat inventor Robert Fulton and his investor Robert Livingston. For all intents and purposes, the region's transportation center, New York Harbor and western Long Island Sound, became an exclusively managed business concern. Connecticut had no legal choice but to operate within its own limited steamboat-centric boundaries.

The newly acquired steamboat *United States* made its maiden voyage to Connecticut in 1822, piloted by the New Haven company's part-owner Captain Benjamin Beecher. Born exactly two years prior to the country's adopting the Declaration of Independence, the Elm City tar had commanded coastal packets during an era when sail ruled the Sound. But the gruff, oath-spewing skipper knew exactly which way the wind blew and that traveling the waves would all too soon be dictated by steam power.[7]

Looking back over his time with the New Haven Steamship Company, he thought how stern a gale it was that the Connecticut shipping firm had survived. Every seafaring man in lower Manhattan shuddered at the tangible prospect of violence the *United States* faced whenever it departed New York Harbor. Maritime law in New York forbade the Connecticut vessel from engaging its own steam engines, thus obliging it to be towed by the schooner *Huntress*. Captain Beecher was in no way pleased about being denied the ability to use his ship's steam power until New York's territorial waters were in his wake. Following behind the straining lines of the lead boat, the *United States* passed through a dangerous gauntlet of Empire State vessels whose malevolent captains set obstacles in Beecher's path and did their best to stove his ship aground. Shouting epithets with raised fists, the ornery Yankee skipper continually managed to evade catastrophe.

Between 1822 and 1824, the *United States* successfully transported people and cargo from New Haven to New York City. However, due to New York's steam-travel restrictions, Captain Beecher was compelled to disembark passengers at Connecticut's westernmost point at Byram Cove. Disgruntled travelers were then forced to cover the remaining twenty-five miles to New York City by stagecoach. This statutorily imposed interference remained enforced until 1824, when the Supreme Court of the United States deemed New York's water domination unconstitutional.

On Saturday, September 11, 1830, Captain Benjamin Beecher was at the helm of the *United States* when Ephraim Wooster boarded for the boat's four o'clock departure. Ephraim leaned back against the railing to glance at his thirty-one fellow passengers, which curiously he realized were all men. The *United States* was an open-decked boat. What would one day become the standard comfort of private cabins on board Long Island Sound steamboats had not yet been introduced. However, Beecher's steamboat did come equipped with a rare pilothouse, the first of its kind, and the inventive captain could seek shelter from inclement weather or find shady relief during summer's blazing hot days. The captain's adversaries mockingly dubbed the rudimentary hut "Beecher's chicken coop."[8] He stood in this "coop" located in the boat's stern while guiding the vessel with a tiller. Since the view forward was obstructed, the pilot relied on a lookout stationed in the bow.

Fare Reduced

And Time Altered.

THE Steam Boats UNITED STATES, Capt. Beecher, and HUDSON, Capt. Sanford, will continue to ply between

N. Haven & N. York:

Leaving New-Haven every		*Leaving New-York every*	
Monday morn'g at	8 o'clk.	Monday morn'g at	8 o'clk.
Monday evening	8 "	Tuesday morning	8 "
Tuesday evening	8 "	Wednesday mor'g	8 "
Wednesday eve'g	8 "	Thursday morning	8 "
Thursday evening	8 "	Friday morning	8 "
Friday evening	8 "	Saturday morning	8 "
Saturday evening	8 "	Saturday aftern'n	4 "

Making seven trips each week. Fare two dollars, and *no charge for meals.* Freight at moderate prices.

POST COACHES

Always in readiness on arrival of the Boats at New-Haven, to convey passengers to Hartford, Boston, and Providence. All baggage at the risk of the owners thereof.

JOEL ROOT, *Agent.*

New-Haven, June 1, 1830 tf51

At a Court of Probate holden at Norfolk, within and for the District of Norfolk, on the

Schedule with Disaster. This September 1830 advertisement announces the *United States* steamship's departures and arrivals. One voyage would never return. *From* Litchfield (CT) Enquirer, *September 2, 1830. Chronicling America: Historic American Newspapers. Library of Congress.*

The sudden loud whistle blast announcing the *United States*' departure startled Ephraim. Its long, shrill reverberation was answered by a deafening double-echo being emitted by two nearby steamboats. Shoving off at the same hour as the New Haven–bound ship were the *Victory* and the *Washington.* Perpetually in competition, the three steamboat captains jockeyed for position. Captain Beecher's craft proved slowest, and the *United States* quickly faded to the back of the pack. Heading north along the East River, the small flotilla approached Hell's Gate, beyond which lay Long Island Sound and, eventually for the *United States,* home at New Haven Harbor's Long Wharf.

Ephraim Wooster was pleasantly surprised to find an acquaintance onboard, New Haven merchant Hiram N. Clarke. The Nutmeggers discussed their day's tidy transactions while ship hands Charles Bowles, Charles Silsby and Benjamin Haskell cupped hands to mouth and bellowed orders to one another. The ship's porter, Alfred Mason, smiled and chatted with passengers while stowing baggage aft. Another New England–bound passenger, Harvey Osman Shelley, was a Guilford, Connecticut sailor returning home from an extended whaling voyage. He sighed aloud as Manhattan slipped calmly passed. The thirty-five-year-old seafarer had been away at sea for nearly half his life. Grinning quietly, Harvey Shelley wondered, "How many years? How many shores?" This day, the seaman gloriously anticipated stomping his old boots on New Haven turf, where he could once more walk arm in arm with old friends.

At approximately 4:15 p.m., Blackwell's Island lay ahead. City hall had acquired the property two years earlier and was putting the land to municipal use: new construction projects included a prison, an almshouse and several hospitals being raised on the narrow finger of former farmland.[9] Merchants Ephraim Wooster and Hiram Clarke paused their conversation and, extending their arms, pointed toward the new construction. Some of the granite buildings were already taking on the shape of medieval fortresses.[10] One day soon, the island would house the world's largest insane asylum. Excusing himself to stretch his legs, Clarke headed aft and strolled away whistling a tune.

Running parallel to Blackwell's Island, both the *Victory* and the *Washington* had taken a route along the western side of the island, while Beecher, with a goal of beating Hell's Gate's ebb tide, advised engineer Slocum to steer for the isle's east coast. The treacherous narrows of Hell's Gate had been given this apt moniker by early Dutch sailors navigating these devilish currents, and the captain of the *United States* was all too familiar with the challenges presented by the dangerous passage.

Passengers leisurely paced the deck of the *United States* watching Blackwell's Island construction projects fade behind. It was 4:30 p.m. now (although, some would later recall it being closer to 5:00). Small matter, though, as time was about to halt aboard this ship. Traveling quite peacefully at its normal speed, the boat was just off the northeast corner of Blackwell's Island when suddenly the hull spasmodically shuddered and the air surrounding the vessel turned to gray molten gas.

Immediately, a deafening explosion convulsed the steamboat. The recently replated flue at the bottom of the boiler ruptured. Chaos reigned. Everywhere was blood, confusion and screaming. (The following details of the disaster have been reconstructed through a variety of contemporary sources.)[11] "The boiler, the boiler," yelled the scrambling crew. Metal and brick from the eight-foot-diameter, twenty-two-foot-long iron cylinder had

What a Cellphone Camera Might Have Recorded on September 11, 1830. Steamboat travel was an exceedingly risky affair. Collisions and boiler explosions claimed countless lives throughout the nineteenth century. *Author's collection.*

instantaneously transformed into a seething blizzard of shrapnel. Far worse was the vast plume of deadly steam. Shredding everything in its path, the death fog propelled missiles of wood and cinder and brick. Originating aft, the blast's effects rapidly expanded forward. In an attempt to escape injury, passengers and crew jumped overboard. The impact of the explosion ruthlessly hurled others from where they had calmly stood only a moment before, thrusting them blindly into the churning East River. Wrapped inside the shrieking pandemonium of flesh-rending steam, stunned survivors who were clinging to the handrails panicked and pulled unsuspecting passengers on deck over the railings and into the swift water below.

When the expanding steam hit Captain Beecher (who had inspected the engine room just minutes earlier), he happened to be collecting fares at the starboard gangway. Both of the skipper's feet were badly scalded, and he was unable to see, having been struck in the left eye with hot debris. Recovering his wits, Beecher shouted commands peppered with profanity, while overseeing rescue efforts. Harvey Shelley, the sailor from Guilford, had been curious about the ship's machinery and, after touring the engine room, paused to chat with the boat's fireman, Martin Wells.[12] Just as the boiler burst, twenty-five-year-old Martin was badly seared and instantly leaped overboard. With flesh dripping from his body, the boiler worker somehow managed to swim ashore to Blackwell's. The Bridgeport resident was carried to the island's almshouse and then transported to Bellevue Hospital at the foot of East 26th Street. Sadly, three days later, on September 14, Martin Wells succumbed to his injuries. Harvey Shelley, cast into the river alongside the fireman, was soon fished from the water. The blast terribly scalded both his legs below the knees. Miraculously, after a nine-month recuperation, Shelley again returned to sea, signing aboard the whaling ship *Connecticut*.[13]

New Haven merchant Hiram Clark was standing near the stern with the boat's porter, Alfred Mason. Dodging the deadly steam, they both launched themselves over the ship's side (witnesses later stated that the force of the explosion viciously propelled the two men together into the river). Neither could swim, unfortunately, and both drowned. Four days later, Clark's body washed ashore on Riker's Island. His remains, ferried by the steamboat *Hudson*, were returned to New Haven, where a large gathering turned out for his funeral, including the local militia, the New Haven Grays. The explosion claimed other lives as well: the ship's first and second cooks, Benjamin Haskell and Charles Silsby, and the waiter, Charles Bowles, all perished. The ship's fifteen-year-old galley hand was lost and never found, though the body of an unidentified teenaged boy was recovered four days later twisting in the fury of Hell's Gate currents. Henry Valentine, a well-known Maiden Lane store owner, survived by vaulting over the handrail and steadfastly remained grasping the railing until the danger had passed. Quite a feat considering the merchant was nearly seventy years old. Charles Hammond, the son of wealthy city landowner and director of the Bank of New York, Abijah Hammond, was only slightly scalded on the hands.

Because tickets were still in the process of being collected, a complete passenger manifest was never realized. There was no certainty about how many men might have been left unaccounted for in the river. At the time, the common, though morbid, method of tallying the number of lost was ascertained by counting hats plucked from the water around a ship's disaster. Of the twelve hats found floating in the East River near the smoldering steamboat, three were claimed, signifying that nine people who had boarded the *United States* died that day.

Rescue efforts were rapid. Once the blast had expended itself and the fire was under control, Captain Beecher ordered the crew to lower a small boat to search for survivors. Nearby, Captain Brooks of the Norwalk steamer the *Citizen*, as well as the Hell's Gate ferry, quickly responded. Later that day, the *Citizen* towed the *United States* back downriver to the wharves of Manhattan's Corlears Hook, just below today's Williamsburg Bridge.

The shockwave from the explosion reached the staff inside Blackwell's Island prison. John O. Woodruff, keeper of the penitentiary,[14] immediately launched all municipal boats at his disposal. Woodruff himself frantically rowed into the river, praying to rescue anyone he might reach in time.

He found Ephraim Wooster. The Derby merchant was in horrendous condition, barely clinging to life. The blast's boiling steam had wizened his body to a reddish pulp. At the moment of the explosion, Ephraim spontaneously sprang over the boat's railing as much to escape the heat as to salve the pain from his burns. But Ephraim landed in the water so close to the ship's hull that it made a tragic situation far worse: he was smashed in the head by the still churning paddlewheel. With flesh falling from Ephraim's torso, jailer Woodruff blanched as he hauled the mangled man into the prison skiff.

Rowing toward shore, the jailer was met by personnel from the adjacent charity hospital still under construction. Woodruff ordered all of the injured to be carried into his own house. Doctors expediently applied their time-tested medical cures to save Wooster: he was pierced and bled. But not even this dubious treatment could torment the Derby man any longer. Nothing could be done to save poor Ephraim. He was dead within fifteen minutes of arriving ashore.

Ironically, after serving as tax collector for the state of Connecticut, Ephraim Wooster would lay in the almhouse on Blackwell's Island unclaimed. He was just three days shy of his sixty-sixth birthday when he died. The Wooster family didn't become aware of Ephraim's fate for another two weeks. With no one claiming Ephraim's decomposing corpse, it took "on a terrific appearance [from] being swelled to an enormous size"[15] and was in no condition to be transported back to Derby. The epitaph in Great Hill Cemetery simply states that his body is buried in New York. In 1921, the East River island where Ephraim is interred was renamed Welfare Island, and the name was again changed in 1973 to Roosevelt Island. Ephraim Wooster's remains are surely still resting somewhere there in an unmarked grave.

THE STORY OF JOSEPH

The strange circumstances surrounding the interment of Ephraim's son, Joseph Davis Wooster, is a mystery. Like his father, he is not buried beneath the Wooster name and dates inside Seymour's Great Hill Cemetery.

Joseph was born in Derby in 1801. He married Mary Tomlinson in January 1831, roughly four months after his father's heartbreaking death. Sadly, Joseph and Mary's union lasted barely more than twelve months. Joseph passed away on January 26, 1832.

The Wooster headstone states that Joseph passed away in New Iberia, Louisiana, and that his body is buried "on the Island of Belize." Questions immediately arise concerning the reason for Joseph's residency deep in Cajun Country. More perplexing is why he was buried in Central America, so far away from where he lived and died! Joseph's single gravestone sentence indicates that his corpse was transported nearly one thousand miles from New Iberia to Belize.

Closer examination of the Wooster epitaph provides a clue. Turns out there's a subtle spelling error in the tombstone's inscription. The confusion arises in the name "Belize."[16] Nineteenth-century Louisiana maps indicate a more practical burial place for Joseph. Once the correct vowel is substituted in the gravestone's lettering (*a* transposed for *e*), it becomes apparent that Joseph D. Wooster is not buried in the nation of Belize but rather on the island of La Balize, a French fort town located at the mouth of the Mississippi River.

Translated from the French, Balize means "seamark" or "beacon." The place-name results from a primitive signal tower established on the island's shore. Dating back more than a century, this tiny hamlet was inhabited by a cadre of fishermen, river pilots, their families and a dazzling influx of brigands and pirates drawn to the island's rowdy saloons. For decades, the miniscule village harbored a well-deserved reputation as one of the most wicked spots along the entire American Gulf Coast.[17] Wooster, having been buried here, just two hundred miles from where he lived in New Iberia, may have been employed as a river pilot connected in some way with coastal shipping.

La Balize's cutthroat legacy was matched only by its dangerous location. Since its establishment during the 1700s, the town had been ravaged by hurricanes and rebuilt repeatedly. The continual cycle of storms and reconstruction compelled this hive of river pilots, and dwindling populace, to depart for a more favorable station. La Balize was eventually abandoned and became little more than a ghost town. The island eventually joined the fate of mythical Atlantis when it sank forever beneath the surge of a devastating hurricane in 1865. Though the island has been swallowed by the Gulf and no longer exists, the area is still referred to as the Balize Delta. In surrealistic defiance to the sea, the island's cemetery refused to surrender. Several gravestones along with a tomb's iron doors somehow reared themselves from the murky depths. Although battered by time and tides, it was reported as late as 1921 that the blasted letters over this crypt's entrance remained legible. They spelled the beginning of the name, "Woo—" Could the unfinished surname mark the burial site of "Woo…ster"? During the 1920s, the crypt's thick metal doors were blasted wide open by dynamite-wielding treasure hunters.[18] It's unknown what, if anything, was discovered or removed. Considering the island's unsavory history, one can only imagine what wealth hides in these underwater sands.

Joseph Wooster's remains must certainly repose in the ground of this sunken village, or perhaps his bones were washed away deep into the Gulf of Mexico. Either way, in the end, it isn't heaps of Naugatuck Valley earth harboring Ephraim and Joseph Wooster. Their vanished remains touch one another in the bottom of the ocean that connects La Balize with New York Harbor.

The faded names and dates chiseled above the Wooster plot within this hillside Seymour cemetery have transformed this cenotaph into a witness stone. Certainly, a witness to the past—but on certain fog-bound nights, when the surrounding woods fall eerily quiet, sometimes the wind inexplicably carries a waft of salt air mingling among the etched graves.

10

SOMETHING WICKED SLITHERS IN PURGATORY

THE WATERTOWN WYRM

The deep woods and coastline of our northeastern United States have provided fertile realms for mysterious and marvelous creatures. Tales abound of giant hirsute humanoids, boat-jarring lake monsters and any number of bizarre beasts whose only clues of existence are delineated in the diffused pawprints or carcasses of dead animals found in their furtive wake. Many are these monsters that dwell in local histories and paranormal books, and many more howl in the computer-glow of urban folklore. But there is at least one New England creature that has literally slithered between the cracks of North America's cryptid heritage: The Watertown Wyrm.

Monstrous serpents have lurked within Connecticut's landscape for centuries. Sacred snake totems are hidden in plain sight. Preserved in New England's meandering stone walls are what some anthropologists point to as "serpent walls." Over generations, these serpentine fieldstone-icons have not only been camouflaged by our reforested countryside but also concealed further within the rocks of colonial farm boundaries and pasture walls.

Connecticut's very topography has been shaped by mythical serpents. Marguerite Allis, in her book *Connecticut Trilogy*, fancifully notes that Indigenous peoples (in what is today's New Haven area) held the belief that the loops of the Quinnipiac River were formed "by the meanderings of a huge dragon which, crawling up through the salt meadows, twisted and turned until, unable either to go on or retreat, it finally died amid the clay banks and the cat-tails. At length the great carcass sank; whereupon the waters rushed in from the bay and made the Dragon's River a path of silver above his bones."[1] Indeed, early Europeans called the lower portion of the thirty-eight-mile-long Quinnipiac waterway "Dragon River" due to the abundance of harbor seals (i.e., sea dragons) at the river's mouth.

Furthermore, a remarkable dragon effigy was uncovered more recently in New England. In 2010, a "serpent stone," allegedly featuring the carved image of what some see as a plumed snake, was found in an undisclosed Roxbury, Connecticut stonewall.[2]

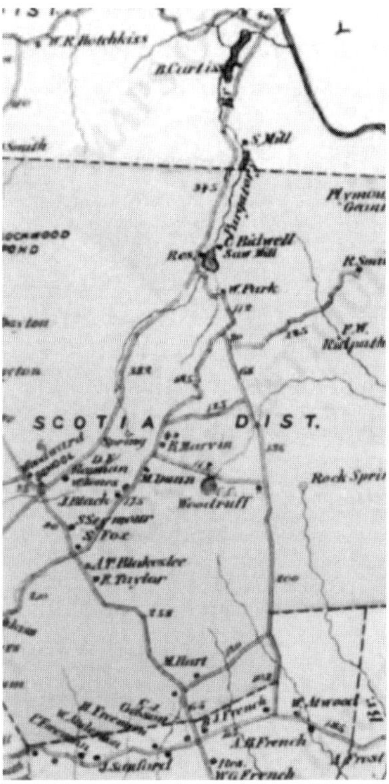

Map of Purgatory. What spawned this Connecticut locale's place-name? Did the rugged landscape and hardscrabble farming help designate the region's moniker? Or could there be an otherworldly connection? *From Town of Watertown, Connecticut, County Atlas of Litchfield, Connecticut, New York:* Published by F. W. Beers and Co., 1874.

There is another legendary snake that must be added to the pantheon of New England serpent lore: for nearly two decades, during the close of the nineteenth century, a monstrous reptile was regularly reported along the roadways, swamps and wooded hillsides of central and western Watertown, Connecticut. Astonished witnesses claimed that this enormous beast stretched twenty-five feet in length or longer. Measuring-stick descriptions of the elusive creature changed as Victorian era technology evolved. Early on, Watertown citizens related that the reptile was as thick as a potbelly "stove pipe," but as the years and snake stories evolved, "his snakeship's" dimensions were compared to the girth of a "telephone pole."

These serpent sightings occurred within very specific Naugatuck Valley boundaries. Known originally as Westbury, the village was renamed Watertown in 1780. Characteristic of many Litchfield County towns, this locale is composed of rugged ledge and scattered swamps, topography that offers slithering creatures a perfect haven. As such, the writhing beast preferred the Nova Scotia District of Watertown. Adding appropriately to the treacherous underworld symbolism of all things fanged and hissing, this serpent was also habitually seen in that lonely part of town known as "Purgatory."

Were visitations by the Watertown Wyrm factual? For those who would say "nay," there are an unbelievable number of snake tales crawling through American folklore. Consider "hoop snakes," which clamp their jaws on their own tails and travel by rolling just like a wheel, or farmers blaming mysterious bovine thefts on cow-suckling serpents. Prior to the 1880s, no one in Watertown subscribed to giant snake stories. Yet over ensuing summers, disturbing tales began to gather traction, especially when "some [Watertown] farmers, whose reputation for veracity is never questioned, told of having actually seen this monster reptile, people began to think there might, after all, be something to it."[3]

One early report occurred in 1889, when an anonymous Watertown farmer went in search of a missing heifer. The lost yearling was valuable, and the dairy owner scoured the hilly countryside. Initially, he figured that the animal had been shot accidentally by a hunter. Imagine the farmer's shock "when the poor creature was discovered [and] there wasn't a whole bone in its body, every bone being crushed as if it had been through a mill."[4] Local farmers were still scratching their heads over this peculiar death when clues to what possibly caused the cow's demise surfaced two years later.

In the autumn of 1891, a hunter wandering the wooded hills west of the Naugatuck River, near the Robert Smith farm, became vexed when his well-trained hunting dog refused to heed his commands. Something enormous was moving through the dense brush and spooked the dog. The frightened hound turned and ran yelping for home. Peering toward the direction of the mysterious crashing sounds, the mesmerized hunter watched thick undergrowth snapping "like pipe stems." Not wanting to come face to face with the unseen source of these destructive noises, the hunter wisely turned tail and joined his retreating dog. Similar accounts that same season resulted in an unspoken decree around Watertown: hunters avoided the area and, according to newspapers, gave "these grounds a wide berth."[5]

Physical evidence of a giant snake was said to be collected the following summer. In late July 1892, townspeople set out to investigate this so-called monster reptile. The search party, at first loud and jocose, were startled into silence upon discovering "the skin of a huge snake, about 10 feet long and 14

½ inches in circumference." The group continued scrutinizing the ground when "further down the hill they found several more pieces, and when laid together, [the snakeskin] measured over 22 feet [in length]."[6] Farmer Smith, who by now wholeheartedly accepted the reality of a giant serpent on his Nova Scotia Hill property, came forward with additional proof: a reptilian hide "at least 25 feet long."[7]

Initially dismissed as ridiculous, these mounting claims now enflamed the fears of the entire Naugatuck Valley. Alarmed citizens felt obligated to protect their families and livestock: enter Judge George Hubert Cowell. The Yale and Columbia Law School graduate was highly respected; he had held various judicial offices and was presently serving as Waterbury's deputy judge of the police court. In the near future, he would be elected to the state legislature. Cowell's word held authority. Folks took heart when the popular public figure resolved to get to the core of the snake situation. The judge generously offered $500 for the elusive mountain eel if captured alive. As for a dead serpent, whomever brought in a snake carcass of twenty feet or more would find themselves $250 richer. Word of the wyrm's worth prompted thirty French Canadians from neighboring Waterbury to thrash through the woods early on Sunday morning, August 7, 1892, hoping to seize "that big Nova Scotia Hill snake."[8] However, no snakeskin trophy, dead or alive, was paraded into town. Oddly enough, Farmer Smith frustratingly exclaimed that the beast was again seen slinking along his property that very August weekend.

Judge George H. Cowell, Monster Hunter. The popular Waterbury judge's bounty offer for the infamous Watertown Wyrm, dead or alive, sparked a hectic quest into Watertown's craggy terrain. *From* Taylor's Souvenir of the Capitol, 1897–1898 *W.H. Taylor, 1897.*

It would be three years before another onslaught of serpent sightings took place. By 1895, local newspapers accepted the reality of the strange snake and commonly referred to the creature as "the old-time terror of Nova Scotia Hill."[9] Soon, that "Terror" would make itself known to Estella Esty. She and her husband, Orrin, owned a farm on Nova Scotia Hill where, during warm weather months, they opened their homestead as a summer resort. The

Estys' delightful boardinghouse comfortably entertained up to ten guests. In late May 1895, with thoughts of readying the place for lodgers who arrived from as far away as New York City, Estella encountered the serpent.

Plodding along Nova Scotia Hill Road, the Esty horse abruptly balked. The thirty-seven-year-old guest house proprietor then witnessed the reason for the animal's sudden fright: gliding across the dirt road in front of her was "an enormous black snake as large around as a stove pipe."[10] The serpent escaped into the bushes. It had been merely a day or two prior that Albert Blakeslee related how he had seen a huge snake in the exact vicinity. Farmer Blakeslee brashly chased the beast into the woods, suspending the pursuit only when he came across a twelve-foot-long section of snakeskin.[11]

One of the most disturbing encounters occurred in Watertown's Curtis Dayton Swamp. Surrounded by dense forest, some portions of the morass were thought to be bottomless according to local legend.[12] Too often, dogs and cattle unlucky enough to wander into this dank region were never seen again. But townsfolk were quick to note that there was something far more foreboding in the swamp than miasmas or treacherous shifting terrain. Newspapers commented, "Of late years hunters have not been able to enter [or] to induce their dogs to enter this swamp at all, and the whole place has been shunned both by man and beast."[13] Everyone avoided Curtis Dayton Swamp. Everyone except for fifty-one-year-old Seth Bassett. The popular Union army veteran was enticed by the dreary site's abundance of tempting berries, including huckleberries, bilberries, blackberries and raspberries. It was a sunny morning in 1896 when the former artilleryman was seen meandering toward Curtiss Dayton Swamp toting a fistful of clanking pails. For weeks, Seth had been intently smacking his lips with thoughts of harvesting the slowly ripening morsels hidden deep inside the swamp. However, Seth would taste only the burn of rising bile once confronted by the frightening Watertown Wyrm.[14]

Neighbors smiled and nodded to Seth that morning as he strolled happily down the road. And it would be these same individuals who, later that day, alarmingly witnessed an unhinged Seth Bassett tearing along Main Street, one shoe flying high in the air behind him.

Startled onlookers reported that "he looked as white as a ghost and that his eyes resembled silver dollars protruding far out of their sockets."[15] It wasn't until hours later that the old cannoneer, who knew the horrors of battle, was able to compose himself and share his terrifying story: After a successful day of foraging berries, Bassett turned homeward when his attention was drawn to a mammoth oak tree several yards in front of him. There was no breeze, yet the tree rocked side to side; Seth recalled that the tree shuddered "as if swayed by a hurricane."[16] The berry picker curiously approached the shaking branches, when he immediately froze, transfixed by the largest snake he had ever seen. The reptile was, in turn, observing a hawk preparing to land in the oak, when the writhing snake lunged from its hidden perch and snatched the bird. Horrified, Bassett watched as the hawk was instantly slaughtered. The stunned man explained that the creature must have been at least thirty feet long, "as coil after coil disappeared in the branches, causing them to snap [under the snake's weight]."[17] Dailies across the country splattered their own inky venom, titling the disturbing incident, "The Connecticut Man Who Saw a Monster Serpent."[18] The *Erie Times-News* noted that the snake, according to Bassett's description, resembled a python and was "altogether different from the one seen time and again on Nova Scotia Hill."[19]

Soon, two Naugatuck Valley legends would find themselves confronting one another in the wild and rocky section of Watertown previously mentioned: Purgatory (according to Watertown History Museum curator Diane Ciba, early in its history, this area was regarded as being "infertile," which may have inspired the dismal locale's name origin. Purgatory Brook still flows dark and brackish through gangly overgrowth. It was in Purgatory during August 1899 that New England's famous wandering hermit, John Brennan, stumbled upon the Watertown Wyrm.

Brennan, who for decades was addressed by such telling nicknames as Johnny o' the Woods and Jack o' the Light, was traversing his accustomed Naugatuck Valley circuit out of Thomaston, Connecticut, when, overcome by fatigue, he secured a place for the night in a Terryville farmer's haystack. Following a fine breakfast provided by the thoughtful farmer, Johnny set out on his pilgrimage toward Watertown. A few miles into his nomadic route, Johnny's barking feet compelled him to stretch out on the roadside near Purgatory Brook. No sooner had Johnny exhaled a relaxing breath when a rabbit darted out from the brush. The cottontail crossed within a few feet of Brennan's supine figure. But it was the terrifying sound that followed the scampering rabbit that alarmed the New England nomad: "a tremendous noise caused by cracking and snapping of branches."[20] Bug-eyed, Johnny sprang to his feet while a twenty-five-foot-long snake, "with [its] head raised about two feet" from the ground, undulated across his path.[21]

His aching feet no longer a consideration, the hobo dashed to the nearest farmhouse, where he breathlessly related the surreal serpent tale.

Johnny o' the Woods. His birth name was John Brennan, and he was one of New England's most enigmatic nineteenth-century wanderers. His circuit through western Connecticut brought him face to slithering face with the Watertown Wyrm. "*John Brennan, full-length portrait, dressed for the role of 'John Pickpenny.'" Photograph, Retrieved from the Library of Congress digital file from b&w film copy negative. http://hdl.loc.gov/loc.pnp/cph.3a38514.*

A search party hastily assembled. Arriving at the location where Johnny had witnessed the beast, the men entered an adjacent ravine. What they discovered forced a speedy retreat. Near the mouth of a cave lay coiled "a huge monster"[22] measuring at least twenty-five feet in length and as thick as a telephone pole. The group's attention focused on an oval swelling set about six feet down from the creature's head; the bulge inside the snake was roughly two feet long, and the direction of its tapering-end pointed toward the snake's tail. The serpent had obviously found Johnny o' the Woods' frightened rabbit.

While this wild story was circulating around town, a reporter with the *Waterbury Daily American* set out to investigate the incoherent claims of the anxious search party.[23] Arriving in Purgatory, about a mile from the exact site where the snake was allegedly seen earlier that day, the newspaperman was stunned by a runaway carriage hurtling down the hill. Leaping on the animal's breeching and straps, the journalist was dragged one hundred yards before the frantic horse finally slowed to a stop. Slumped at the base of the driver's bench, a woman lay unconscious. Her two children, ages five and eight, cried inconsolably. Once the carriage's owner was revived, she related a terrifying experience. Heading toward Watertown, the family pet had spotted something ahead of them lurking in the roadside brush; their large Newfoundland dog dashed out of the wagon to chase the unseen quarry. Roused from its hiding spot, the snake bolted across the road. The slithering animal was much too close to the moving carriage for the driver to effectively veer aside and avoid colliding with the swiftly moving shadow. The conveyance crashed into the monster snake with such a force that the driver was knocked senseless. Not quite sure what to make of the dazed woman's story, the reporter surveyed the scene. The two children were sobbing inside the carriage, and the dog, which by now had returned, cowered on the ground between the wagon's wheels. The skeptical reporter inspected the vehicle; the right side of the wagon was heavily damaged, and the undercarriage rods were bent and twisted. Whatever might have been run over was obviously a massive object.

Another strange incident occurred on the same Purgatory road in 1900.[24] A well-to-do Boston family was enjoying an extended summer tour of the upper Naugatuck Valley when they too encountered the Watertown Wyrm. The husband, wife and son, along with a coachman, wound along the hilly road not far from today's Black Rock State Park. Sections of the lane were sandy, and the carriage travel was slow, but no one was in a hurry. The two horses pulling the stately rig suddenly froze in the middle of the lane. Not even the coachman's encouraging words coaxed the horses onward. When he applied the whip, the animals began to buck and kick. At that moment, a giant serpent, measuring more than twenty-five feet, whipped at "lightning speed" across the road, in front of the dumbfounded family. The Bostonian noted, "I have never seen anything in my life that could get over the ground as rapidly as that serpent." Determined to make a trophy of this marvelous specimen, the gentleman grabbed his Winchester and was about to pursue the escaping monster when his agitated wife protested. She demanded that the coach be turned around and gallop as far away as possible from Watertown. This the husband refused. Cradling his rifle, he guardedly stepped down from the plush vehicle and walked slowly down the road in front of their coach. All was silent. At one point, the husband hailed a passing hay wagon in order to warn the young driver about their wild encounter with the serpent. The open-mouthed farm boy turned ashen and stared off into oblivion. Soon after, the father clambered back on board the carriage and settled in beside the coachman. Both kept an outlook for any odd movement in the surrounding brush. After traveling a few miles up the steep grade, the family finally stopped to rest at a stranger's house. Here, the homeowner relayed to the wide-eyed Bostonians that Purgatory's surrounding woods were the longtime lair of a giant serpent.

Certainly, it is frightening enough to confront a massive reptile in the wilderness. But it is something altogether much more terrifying to think that such a creature could slither inside one's own home. That is exactly what happened on Sunday, June 15, 1902, when Joseph Keilty, a clerk at Atwood's Drugstore, arrived with a delivery at the home of Dr. Walter Seward Munger in Watertown.[25] The apothecary worker, as was his custom, knocked on the door and nonchalantly entered Munger's house. The young fellow stood in disbelief. There in the main hall an enormous snake writhed around a rolled carpet. The clerk grabbed a heavy household tool and dispatched the fanged intruder. Though it was not the Wyrm of legend, the Munger household

Above: Another Sleepless Night at Doctor Munger's DeForest Street Home. On June 15, 1902, a giant serpent was discovered inside the doctor's Watertown residence. *Author's collection.*

Opposite: When the Circus (and Snakes) Came to Town. Traveling menageries, like the one included with the John B. Doris Circus, attracted audiences throughout western Connecticut. Could an escaped python explain the existence of the Watertown Wyrm? *Waterbury Daily Republican, May 10, 1886.*

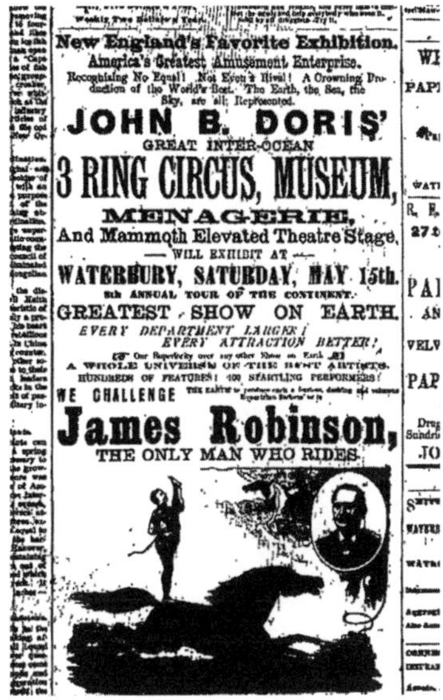

assuredly spent more than one sleepless night wondering under which bed another monster snake might lurk.

Eventually, the Watertown Wyrm slithered into the chinks and cracks of shadowy fable before being utterly forgotten. Was this Connecticut creature a survivor from the prehistoric past, a throwback to an ancient reptile or an altogether new and therefore unidentified species? But there might be another more plausible source for the snake's presence in the Naugatuck Valley. Could an exotic carnival creature have absconded while passing through Watertown? Some contemporaries focused on the possibility that a few years prior "two or three" enormous boa constrictors may have escaped from a traveling circus.[26] Such cases have been documented.

One humongous fork-tongued vertebrate escaped from Barnum & Bailey's winter quarters in Bridgeport during 1895, only to be found twenty miles away in Darien, Connecticut.[27] The *Norwalk Hour*, in 1912, printed a story about a twelve-foot anaconda being killed in Stamford after the circus had departed its show grounds on Summer Street.[28] In addition to traveling carnivals, wayward snakes have been frightening folks throughout the Northeast for a long time. A rhumba of rattlesnakes broke free from a delivery crate in the Rockville, Connecticut Adams Express office at the turn of the last century.[29] The rattlers had been shipped to a country fair for exhibition purposes and were being returned to a showman in Winsted. In another instance, children were warned to stay indoors when a twenty-foot, two-hundred-pound Indian python wiggled its way out of an exhibit near Rochester, New York, in 1930.[30]

On the other hand, there were many Naugatuck Valley inhabitants who thought that the existence of the Watertown Wyrm was just a bunch of snake oil. These herpetology doubters summed up Watertown's whopping snake stories as a monstrous joke. Or, they figured, the scaly rumors were being employed as part of a disinformation campaign aimed at keeping prying fingers away from prime berry-picking spots. "It seems so funny that these large reptiles are only seen [during the harvesting time] of the year," wrote a person using the pseudonym "Blackberry Grounds" in an 1899 letter to the

Waterbury Daily American.[31] With an inky smirk, that anonymous letter writer observed how these Watertown snake tales always seemed to occur "when [trespassing] children are picking berries."

Just tell that to the distraught farmers searching for all those missing dogs and vanished sheep.[32]

11
The Devil's Address

Pleased to meet you. Hope you guess my name.
—The Rolling Stones, "Sympathy for the Devil"

Connecticut has hosted a litany of dark and diabolical locales: brimstone-sizzling sites such as Satan's Ridge in New Hartford, Tophet Road in Roxbury and the Devil's Hopyard in East Haddam provide just a few unholy examples. By default, our state's rivers also cradle a Satanic connection. The waters of the Naugatuck River, which flow into the Housatonic, eventually mingle with the moon-shadowed waves once known as The Devil's Belt (the strange appellation attached to colonial maps indicating Long Island Sound). It would appear that cloven-hooved Old Nick found Connecticut an all-too-familiar stomping ground. However, there is another sinister site that must be inventoried with his satanic majesty's geographic grimoire, an ungodly place so loathed by Naugatuck Valley residents that the town fathers officially obliterated Beelzebub's own blazing "home address" from local Seymour-Oxford maps: the forbidden location ominously christened as "Hell Lane."

So, where in the heck was Hell Lane? Debate has raged over the path's nefarious route for one hundred years. All parties agreed at the time that the road was situated somewhere along the outermost reaches of Seymour, Connecticut. Pinpointing its whereabouts today is made even more difficult due to the work of early twentieth-century politicos who successfully expunged all references to the foreboding genius loci.

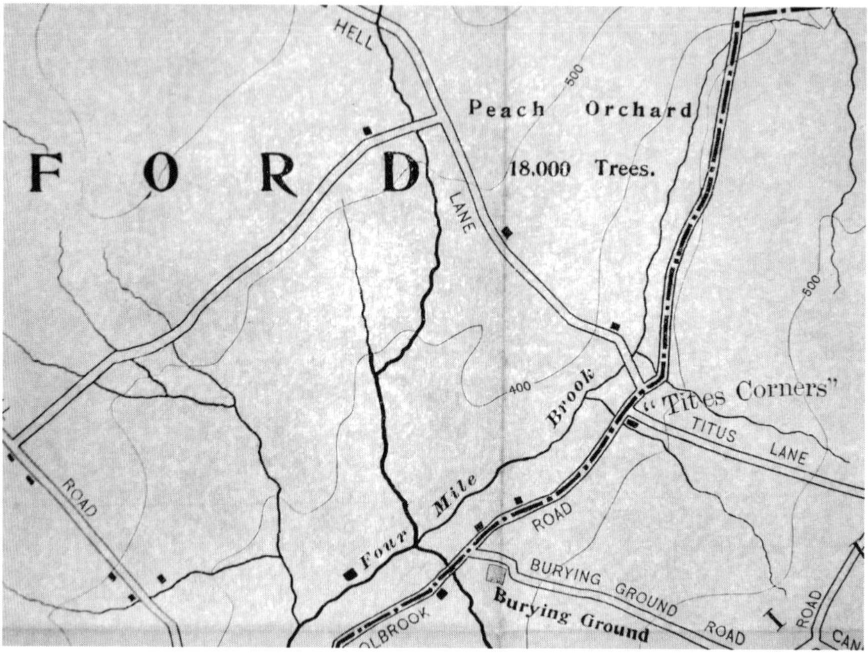

Highway to Hell (Lane). *Map of Seymour, New Haven County, Connecticut 1902.* This map illustrates the devil's address as occupying the Oxford side of the border. Formerly displayed in the Seymour Town Clerk's Office, the map has been removed for safekeeping. *Courtesy of Seymour Town Hall, Town Clerk's Office. Photographed by Michael J. Bielawa, taken November 13, 2019.*

Nowadays, Hell Lane is more forgotten than feared. Erasing a name, though, does not readily remove its memory. Or its mysterious legacy…

Hell Lane loomed above the Naugatuck River on the far side of Great Hill in the shadowy vale separating Seymour from Oxford. There's always been something amiss about the old road where October's moon reshapes the stone walls of forgotten builders.

What brought folks to an area that they eventually felt compelled to dub Hell Lane? During the colony's earliest days, Great Hill held sway as the region's dynamic hub. Accessed from the Housatonic River and holding command over the Naugatuck, this six-hundred-foot highland was soon populated with homes and schools, mills and tanneries.

But Great Hill would not long remain a viable economic force. Events cast the place as a sort of magnet for the bizarre, and during the ensuing decades, odd things occurred up on Great Hill.[1] A glowing meteor crashed deep in the woods at the summit.[2] Insanity visited various families.[3] There were reports of strange and sudden deaths. Josiah Nettleton, who lived on Hell Lane, once found it necessary to apply tar to cover a mysterious mutilation he found on the side of one of his cows.[4] And terrifying situations still have not ceased. In 2001, specialists from the Center for Disease Control wandered the hill in hazmat suits trying to figure out how deadly anthrax had arrived in a Great Hill Road mailbox.

Ninety-nine years prior to the anthrax case, the history, *Seymour, Past and Present*, published an invaluable list of local roads.[5] The authors even provided a perplexing set of directions to hell; W.C. Sharpe and his colleagues placed Hell Lane along today's Holbrook Road.[6] They then extended it westward into Oxford, mirroring the current Moose Hill Road. However, the exact location of Hell Lane was hardly affixed to a map with the devil's red-hot trident. There were conflicting claims as to where the road began and ended: in 1954, Norman Litchfield, who penned *History of Christ Church, Quaker Farms in Oxford, Connecticut*, identified Hell Lane as *just* the path leading into Oxford (not including the Seymour stretch);[7] a century earlier, the *Derby Journal* of November 21, 1850, also indicated that this same Oxford-bound section was *solely* Hell Lane.[8] Yet in between these claims in 1902, the (Ansonia) *Evening Sentinel* asserted that this devilish road was *only* the present-day Holbrook Road and that the extension previously understood to lead into Oxford was a road monikered Rogue's Alley (Rogue's Alley is now shown on maps to be the aforementioned Moose Hill Road.).[9] Nothing is right about this place—even the coordinates are "hellish" to pin down.

Theories abound on how Hell Lane got its name. Perhaps it is these very directions that provide the simplest explanation: the corner where Holbrook Road takes a sharp right angle turn onto Moose Hill Road was once known as "Ell" Road, and over time, this name could have been corrupted into the more colorful "Hell" misnomer.[10]

Popular oral tradition perpetuates the profane Hell Lane title as being derived from a disreputable drinking establishment. Located near today's Route 188 traffic circle, there once stood a roadhouse with a debauched reputation. So raucous was the notoriety of this tavern (located adjacent to the little Methodist church) that the saloon went by the name of Hell House.[11] There was a time when the road from Woodbury, Roxbury and Washington to New Haven made this combination roadhouse-hotel a convenient halfway tarrying destination. Any teamster interested in getting a fix of earthly pleasures need only take the well-travelled Hell Lane to revel in the sinful Hell House.[12]

At some point in the annals of Hell Lane, whose boisterous denizens proudly called themselves "Hell Laners," an Episcopal minister concocted the notion of saving the rough-and-tumble hillside community. The unbridled

Lane-folk repelled and rebelled against this intrusion and compelled the minister to quickly depart, along with his unwelcome blessings. Once off the hill, the exasperated holy man mopped his brow and sighed that this place had never been more fittingly labeled.[13]

One of the inveterate rabble-rousers of Hell Lane was the proprietor of Hell House, a fellow known as "Cap'n Gillett."[14] Carousing in a Derby saloon late one night, he inquired of the town bell ringer, Old Todd, if he was available for hire. Gillett explained that his horse rode more swiftly when serenaded by music. Todd was offered a silver dollar if he'd be inclined to help speed the steed, whereupon the drunken Cap'n Gillett mounted his horse and raced off to Hell Lane. It was midnight when Old Todd happily earned his pay and clanged the Derby academy's bell—rousting the town's citizens from their slumber and sending them running pell-mell into the streets to answer the emergency call.[15] The Hell Laner Gillett howled with laughter the entire way back to Great Hill.

Another widely circulated tale about the origin of Hell Lane's name focuses on the inordinate number of resident tipplers. Hoisting a jug on one's elbow was a passion readily exercised around the Oxford border, what with the plethora of cider brandy distilleries.[16] Apparently, Hell Lane was considered by some as a bucolic nineteenth-century skid row, attracting a population of torpid wastrels.

An additional place-name story centers on a local legend about two industrious Hell Laners intent on making their fortunes. The duo went about collecting hemlock timber for constructing coffins, all the while boasting that their craftmanship was so special, and since they were manufacturing caskets for the impious Hell Lane community, they naturally hoped "to make a good showing in hell."[17]

There is yet another darker reason for Hell Lane's name that has never before been brought to light: Great Hill's Spiritualism. Apparently, this highland and its surrounding area had long summoned acolytes intrigued with delving into the ghost world. Rumors of cultish spiritual enclaves, odd chants, and strange incantations echoed within the hill's ancient hovels. A lonely clapboard farmhouse, a relic of colonial times, aptly painted red and set back on Hell Lane near the intersection of Holbrook and Moose Hill Roads (Hell Lane central) was once occupied by James Beardsley (also spelled Beardslee). A farmer by trade, Beardsley "like many others, had a local reputation [for spirit conjuring] and his home became the center for the gathering of the spiritualists of the mystical order," revealed the historian W. C. Sharpe.[18] Might the reference to "many others" be an indication of the occult mindset of Great Hill dwellers? A page from *Seymour, Past and Present* includes a menacing commentary: "It is not stated as to [whether the Great Hill Spiritualists] communication [was] with the spirits of darkness, or with spirits of light."[19] Beardsley died in 1860 at the age of eighty-four. His body rests in Great Hill Cemetery off Hell Lane. Strangely enough, the cracks crawling across his gravestone resemble a dowsing rod, a divining stick unnervingly pointing directly toward Beardsley's remains.

One occultist wandering wind-strewn Great Hill definitely had communication with darker spirits.[20] Samuel Sly—the exorcist-murderer "Uncle Sammy," as he was widely known—was born in Huntington, Connecticut, in February 1803. A jumbled timeline finds Sly, at about age thirty, working at the Stratford Point Lighthouse. Uncle Sammy had a falling out with the lighthouse keeper and needed a new home. Eerily, Sly would later testify that a disembodied voice commanded him to venture up the Naugatuck River to Seymour's Spiritualist stronghold.[21] The mystic lived on Great Hill, where he gathered herbs for potions and sought the numinous powers of witch hazel.

At some point during Sly's supernal journeys, he escorted his older half sister Rhoda Wakeman to New Haven, where they sold magic concoctions from a shanty at the Grove Street Cemetery. Samuel and his sister would soon write a strange and appalling page in New England's supernatural history. Uncle Sammy was a fervent devotee of the infamous Wakemanite cult—a pseudo-religion founded in the first half of the nineteenth century by his aforementioned sister, Rhoda Wakeman. Widow Wakeman was the self-proclaimed prophetess of a maniacal congregation consisting of New Haven County outcasts and simple backwoods laborers. Rhoda decreed to her followers that she had previously died (murdered by her husband, she claimed) decades earlier and then returned from heaven as an empowered deity. One of the prophetess's holy writs stated that should she die again, the world would be destroyed. Imagine the enclave's consternation when Rhoda vehemently asserted that a demon inhabited the body of a Hamden mechanic and fellow Wakemanite, Justus Matthews. Unknown to Matthews, Rhoda announced that this evil entity meant to do her fatal harm. The Wakemanites determined that their only rational course of action was to cast the evil spirit out of Matthews. The ceremony would take place in New Haven. Matthews was bludgeoned to death by Samuel Sly in the early hours of Christmas Eve 1855. The carefully chosen weapon was a two-and-a-half-foot long witch hazel staff, an enchanted wood according to Uncle Sammy, perfect to evict infernal spirits. Completing the violent exorcism, Sly gashed his victim's throat with a small pocketknife and then repeatedly stabbed a large fork into poor Matthews's chest. Soon afterward, the Wakemanites were rounded up and brought to trial. Samuel Sly and Rhoda Wakeman were judged not guilty due to reason of insanity. Being found criminally insane got them both incarcerated for the remainder of their natural lives. Uncle Sammy died in the New Haven County Jail in July 1865,[22] convinced that he was the biblical prophet Elijah.

Hell Lane would survive another half century. Eventually, the Spiritualists vanished like a nightmare at dawn. Yet it wasn't the morning sun that had dispersed the shadow of the lane. The route was officially obliterated by a government committee. At Seymour's annual town meeting held in October 1901, newly elected officials authorized a group of town fathers to rename the local roads.[23] Across the town line from Seymour, Oxford citizens applauded the idea and decided to alter their own devilish bend of road: Rogue's Alley. Since the Hale Coleman Orchard, one of the state's largest, was situated near Rogue's Alley, the route was rechristened as Orchard Street.[24] By early November 1901, the Seymour Committee on Roads reached their decision: the dismal Hell Lane moniker was altered to the wholesome Holbrook Road (Holbrook being an important family in Seymour's history, particularly on Great Hill).

New maps were carefully prepared following the recommendations of the Seymour officials. The charts would incorporate detailed information from the federal government's geological surveys. Announcements prior to its publication celebrated the map and the renaming of multiple roads. Months later, during the summer of 1902, the anxiously awaited charts finally arrived from the printer in Buffalo, New York. The maps were eagerly unfolded in the selectmen's room and...imagine the shock of the townsfolk when they discovered boldly inked on the Seymour border, the supposedly deposed "Hell Lane" still burned in black ink across the parchment. The maps were returned for correction.[25]

What's in a name? The "Holbrook Road" designation apparently *didn't* catch on in 1902. The route was known as Oxford Road from 1914 through 1952. Holbrook Road appears as a listing in the Seymour Town Directory commencing in 1953. Moose Hill Road had its official premiere in Seymour Town Directories with the 1948 edition.

Who, or better yet, *what* caused the "hellish" map error? Was it a publisher's mistake? Or perhaps the handiwork of an inexperienced printer's devil? Or could it be a mischievous tradition-bound Seymourite? No one could answer. All anybody knew was that Hell Lane would not go away quietly. Newspapers around the state poked an editorial pitchfork at Seymour's map debacle. The devious devil, it seemed, got the gleeful final click of hooves.

PART III
OMEN ANTIQUITATUM

12
The Summoning

Christmastide, with its lengthening nights, inviting fireside chimneys and warm wassail, offers the ideal season for sharing ghost stories....But, according to several newspaper accounts, the following is a factual encounter with something otherworldly that occurred one winter's eve in the Naugatuck Valley...

John Connors retired to bed at eleven o'clock one frigid December night in 1894. Walking upstairs, the fifty-something-year-old paused on the stair landing in order to gaze outside the window. He shuddered with the cold pouring through the glass panes. Waves of snow rolled over the countryside. It was going to be quite a storm, Connors thought to himself and continued up the stairway of his Derby, Connecticut home. Within an hour, John Connor's wife would enter their bedchamber—only to find it empty. The lantern she held at arm's length was of little use; its dim illuminance merely coaxed more shadows from the corners rather than alleviate the chilly darkness. Oddly, she noted, nothing in the room suggested anything unusual. In a surreal tableau, John's clothes were folded carefully and placed ever so neatly near the dresser. The bed's thick quilt was turned over a bit, creating a cozy fabric entrance, as if a person were just about to climb within the inviting warm sheets, yet no one had. Perplexed, Mrs. Connors called downstairs. Maybe John had become occupied in the cellar? No reply came forth. The rest of the family, shaken by their mother's bellowing appeals, were now awake. The Connors clan ventured from room to room, searching everywhere. Yet their patriarch was nowhere to be found.[1]

Mrs. Connors piled warm furs atop a heavy jacket and set out into the freezing night in order to summon the constable. Once on the scene, the lawman repeated a quick search of the house. Nothing. Alarmed, the constable, along with the Connors children, trudged from house to house calling their neighbors to organize a search party. Shouts for the missing John Connors refused to pierce the muffled winter air. The searchers' beckoning voices wrestled with the harsh blowing snow and, unheeded, were carried away by the swirling crystal daggers of the consuming storm.

Soon the small band set off deeper into the woods and proceeded down the snow-covered road. No one would say as much, but the older folk held little hope that they would find the vanished man alive, who by now was wandering within the maw of a December gale. The search proved useless, as nothing could be tracked in the raging blow. Overnight, the valley countryside was coated with twelve inches of snow.

But lo! When dawn arrived, John Connors was found under the strangest of circumstances. As the possible list of the lost man's logical whereabouts narrowed, searchers decided it might be prudent to visit the Irishman's far-flung relations, no matter how distant they might reside.

John Connors's uncle Michael McEnerney lived about seven miles away in the town of Orange. It was here that the shocked volunteers discovered John Connors.[2] Barefoot and nearly naked, John Connors had arrived at McEnerney's front door in the middle of the night, where he collapsed a few steps inside his uncle's vestibule. Fevered and barely conscious, John Connors was placed in a nearby bedroom. The local doctor, in fact, was just taking leave of the McEnerney house as the search party appeared. The physician tipped his fur homburg to the group of searchers who were hastily approaching the McEnerney front steps.

With a reassuring nod, Uncle Michael greeted the newly arriving searchers. He explained just how disconcerting it was to respond to someone pounding on his door during the bleakest hours of the night, only to find his unclothed nephew, frozen and disoriented. John Connors, McEnerney related, had left his Derby home without a single word to his wife or children. Obviously, John Connors must have experienced some kind of debilitating mental anguish. Later, commenting on the episode, the authorities would indeed label John Connors's midnight run "a temporary aberration of the mind." [3]

More stunning, however, was McEnerney's detailed and bewildering account of his nephew's seven-mile barefoot run during a blinding December squall. Those assembled were anxious to hear what exactly had transpired prior to John Connors crumpling into an icy puddle inside the McEnerneys' foyer. Before losing consciousness, John Connors breathlessly shared the following tale with his uncle: "I was readying myself for bed. The time was exactly 11 o'clock.[4] While flipping the bed covers, I suddenly became paralyzed by what stood before me. There, in front of my eyes, some sort of mist was materializing! The fog quickly formed into a human shape…an apparition!" John Connors's uncle paused and nervously swallowed, then continued the story as it was related to him. "My nephew did not recognize the mysterious entity standing there in the middle of his Derby bedroom. But he did explain, just as he fell unconscious, that the wraith-like thing provided a message.

"The apparition said, 'Your aunt…is seriously ill. Go to her.'"[5] Michael McEnerney shook his head at how bizarre the statement sounded, "This is the reason why my nephew raced here. To care for his aunt."

John Connors had been found. And was safe. Satisfied, if not a little confounded by the ordeal, the gathered men, now warmed by hot coffee and biscuits, prepared to leave the McEnerney house. The homeowner bid them to please depart as quietly as possible. One member of the search party whispered, "Oh, we have no mind to disturb John Connors. He is a good man, and we are happy he is safe with family." McEnerney slowly looked back, turning his gaze judiciously on each wind-burned face in the group, "No, no, my friends…I bid you please be silent on behalf of my wife, Mrs. McEnerney. She suffered a stroke late last night before John arrived."[6]

13

Living Apparitions

A Doppelgänger's Forewarning

More chilling are the tales of the doppelganger being the harbinger or omen of death.
—Paul Tremblay, Disappearance at Devil's Rock, *2016*

The ensuing narrative has been verified through a number of sources. The incident portrayed here originally came to the author's attention while perusing issues of *The Spiritual Telegraph*, a nineteenth-century paranormal newspaper. This unique weekly journal collected and reported on supernatural events, with a particular focus on psychical interaction with the dead.

There was a time, now long faded from memory, when Connecticut loomed as one of the world's main portals to the Beyond. Our state, certainly known for its staunch Yankee habits, surprisingly coalesced a weird cabal of seers, diviners, prophets and psychics all claiming a rather disconcerting ability to communicate with the dead. The burgeoning industrial city of Bridgeport served as a spectacular outpost situated on the cusp of the Unknown.

One of Spiritualism's principal nineteenth-century acolytes guiding the mystically enlightened along this occult path was Bridgeport resident Samuel Byron Brittan. Oddly, despite Brittan's nationally recognized supernatural investigations and transcendent activities, little biographical documentation exists about the metaphysical man.[1]

Samuel was born on August 13, 1815, in Phillipston, Massachusetts. Already keen on exploring the larger world, the precocious seven-year-old Brittan ran away from home. Following eight years of wandering, he found himself apprenticed to a Brooklyn carriage maker. Finding no taste for the manufacturing trades, Brittan embarked on a teaching career while simultaneously studying for the priesthood. In late 1840, he was taken into fellowship as a Christian minister by the New York Association of Universalists and in August 1841 was ordained. During the next few years, he served as a pastor in Danbury, Connecticut, as well as Albany, New York, before settling (in 1845) in the recently incorporated city of Bridgeport.

Around this same time, Brittan became seriously ill. Waking after a twelve-day coma (some called it a trance), the reverend renounced Universalism and became a focused devotee of the Spiritualist-mesmerist Andrew Jackson Davis. Known as the Poughkeepsie Seer, Davis is regarded as one of America's earliest mystics.[2] Joining Davis's innermost circle, Brittan acquired occult knowledge and confidently sought communication with the world beyond the Veil.

Mystic, Samuel Byron Brittan. Brittan (1815–1883) is one of Connecticut's earliest and most famous chroniclers of the supernatural. In addition to his forays into poltergeist-populated realms, Brittan attested that he held a conversation with a friend's doppelgänger while staying in the Naugatuck Valley. *From S.B. Brittan* Man and His Relations: Illustrating the Influence of the Mind on the Body: The Relations of the Faculties to the Organs, and to the Elements, Objects and Phenomena of the External World, *W.A. Townsend, 1864. HathiTrust.*

From 1847 to 1849, Brittan (who by now was addressed interchangeably as both Reverend and Professor) became the editor-in-chief of Davis's own popular spiritual newspaper, *The Univercoelum*. Articles expounded on the strange world of clairvoyance, dreams and mediumistic trance states. Eventually, a disgruntled Brittan parted ways with Davis due to the latter's lack of nineteenth-century moral sensibilities. It appears that the Poughkeepsie Seer, who at the time was staying in the Bridgeport home of Brittan, had invited a married, though separated, woman (identified as Catherine De Wolf) to live with him under the reverend's roof. Antebellum New England, while tolerant of communing with dead men, was more shocked and far less forgiving in matters of cohabitating with a living woman. Such gross indecency, the good reverend could not and would not abide.

Brittan continued his lifelong journey into the paranormal with his own psychic periodicals. The professor went on to edit *The Shekinah* (a monthly journal devoted to "the Spiritual Nature and Relations of Man" that was published in Bridgeport) and later was co-publisher and editor of the influential New York magazine *The Spiritual Telegraph*. During his sundry travels, Brittan graduated with a degree from Penn Medical University,[3] touring the nation as a well-recognized Spiritualist lecturer and healer.

Throughout his life, Brittan would witness a plethora of paranormal episodes. One of the strangest and most unnatural recurring situations for the reverend relates to his encounters with doppelgängers. Literally meaning "double-walker" in German, these entities can be defined as an individual's perfectly replicated shadow-twin. Brittan's experiences with doppelgängers prompted the reverend to theorize that human souls are capable of leaving the body during life and journeying to places far removed from a person's flesh-and-blood shell. One curious doppelgänger incident occurring in the Naugatuck Valley was documented by Brittan and appears in the September 23, 1854 issue of *The Spiritual Telegraph*. In this article, the reverend relates that sometime during the late 1840s, he had found himself confronted by what he termed a soul-wandering "living apparition" while residing "in the Valley of the Naugatuck."

Brittan was enjoying a visit at the home of his Ansonia friend William Godley Creamer,[4] a Naugatuck Valley entrepreneur who owned a stove and metal shop located near the Derby railroad station on the east bank of the Naugatuck River Bridge.[5] Creamer, a mechanical genius, was on the verge of developing a new railroad car braking system. His invention would save the lives of an untold number of train passengers across the country. Known as the "Creamer Safety Brake," the revolutionary device generated a vast fortune for the inventor. Soon enough, with his brake registered in the patent office and with wealth in pocket, William Creamer departed his Ansonia residence. The inventor would soon go on to purchase two new homes, one in natty New Haven and the other situated closer to his newly formed manufactory in Brooklyn, New York.

The Spiritual Telegraph article of 1854 relates how, just prior to sunrise, Brittan awoke in Creamer's former Ansonia house. Contemplating the prospect of a fine breakfast, what with the kitchen's delicious aromas rising to meet him upstairs, the reverend-professor quickly finished tidying his chamber. Turning to exit the bedroom, Brittan was startled by a person standing silently in front of him. Behind the stranger, the chamber's single door remained shut, and Brittan acknowledged that he heard no one enter his room.[6]

Quite suddenly, the identity of this soundless visitor dawned on the professor. It was an old acquaintance of Brittan's and a fellow Spiritualist: Joseph Trowbridge Bailey.[7] Brittan realized that the man standing opposite him could not physically be here in Ansonia or anywhere near the Naugatuck Valley. Bailey was a well-known Philadelphia jeweler who Brittan knew was not scheduled for a local visit. Nor was Bailey supposed to be anywhere inside the boundaries of Connecticut. Brittan interpreted this vison as the embodiment of a doppelgänger or, in Brittan's own parlance, "a living apparition." So, what could be the reason for this doppelgänger's presence? Brittan, as the unabashed explorer of the Unknown, was ecstatic for the opportunity to interview the astral image of Joseph Trowbridge Bailey.

Speaking first, jeweler Bailey's "living apparition" cryptically stated, "I shall call on you tomorrow." Intrigued, Brittan responded, "What is to be done tomorrow?" The Bailey phantom repeated, "Remember! I shall call on you tomorrow." The Spiritualist editor was adamant in discerning the reason for Bailey's statements, "Friend, will you explain the object of this strange interview? Tell me, what is to occur on the morrow?" Ready to depart, the psychic-image of Joseph Trowbridge Bailey turned toward the door. Alarmed that he might lose the ability to converse with a living apparition, Brittan tactfully implored, "Stay, friend! Explain the object of this mysterious visit." As if in a dreamscape, Bailey's twin visage exasperatingly avoided any direct response but continued rambling in a barely audible whisper.

As the doppelgänger faded from sight, Brittan carefully pieced together bits of the one-way conversation and came to the realization that the Bailey doppelgänger was actually discussing a mutual friend—a person Brittan would later identify only as "Mr. F——."[8] Most of the doppelgänger's hushed comments were faint, but Brittan distinctly heard Bailey's last words; the jeweler's corporeal ghost quite plainly declared, "A dark cloud has settled down over the earthly destiny of that man." With that sentence completed, Bailey's living apparition vanished.

Pressing business obliged Brittan to board the New York & New Haven Railroad the following day. With the surreal visitation distinctly in mind, Brittan's occult adventure took an even stranger twist. Imagine the reverend's utter shock when he discovered the living Bailey on the same train. The jeweler related how he was traveling from Boston, where he'd been occupied during the past few days (far from Ansonia, Connecticut). Brittan opted not to alarm his colleague or lead Bailey into any contrived dialogue that would result in a preconceived conversation, so he decided to avoid mentioning the spectral visit that had occurred the previous morning. Without any prompting, Joseph Trowbridge Bailey suddenly commenced discussing the "misfortunes" of their mutual friend, "Mr. F," whom the doppelgänger had noted in his hushed harangue.

Expressing only concern for their ill friend's situation, Brittan suppressed any demonstrative gasp or word that would expose his recent weird experience. Their conversation at an end and with Bailey's station approaching, the jeweler took his leave, wishing Brittan a fond farewell. Stepping away, Joseph Trowbridge Bailey abruptly turned to face Brittan; employing the exact phrase his own living apparition had imparted the previous morning, Bailey bluntly stated aloud, "A dark cloud has settled down over the earthly destiny of that man."

What was the meaning of this Naugatuck Valley astral visitation? Motivated by the eerie experience, Brittan would share the scene in *The Spiritual Telegraph*. Years later, the reverend re-created this particular supernatural episode (among others) in a chapter Brittan titled, "Apparitions of the Living" in his metaphysical work, *Man and His Relations: Illustrating the Influence of the Mind on the Body*. The Bridgeport Spiritualist calmly reasoned that "the soul is not necessarily confined by its corporeal restraints to any specific locality; but…it is free to traverse the world….Indeed, in some essential sense, the soul leaves the body, and makes excursions into remote regions."[9] Thus was the entity Samuel Byron Brittan witnessed one morning as the sun rose over the "Valley of the Naugatuck" in Ansonia, Connecticut.

NOTES

1. Ghosts of Waterbury

1. "Died," *Waterbury Weekly Republican*, May 14, 1886.
2. "What Is It? Fear and Trembling Caused in the Hearts of Many Residents of the Fourth Ward by a Supposed Ghostly Visitor," *Waterbury Daily Republican*, May 28, 1886.
3. "A Waterbury Ghost," *Hartford Daily Courant*, May 31, 1886.
4. "What Is It?"
5. "What Is It?"
6. "What Is It?"
7. "What Is It?"
8. "What Is It?"
9. "Not a Ghost: An Explanation of the Shearon House Noises," *Waterbury Daily Republican*, June 3, 1886.
10. "Factory 'Ghost': Sensation Created at Waterbury—This 'Spirit' Talks," *Times-Union* (Albany, NY), March 4, 1901.
11. "Factory 'Ghost' Talks," *Waterbury Democrat*, March 4, 1901. (This Waterbury article states that they received the supernatural information about Samuel Lukes from the *New York Herald*.)
12. "'Ghost' in a Waterbury Factory," *Stamford Daily Advocate*, March 8, 1901.
13. Oliver E. Carruth, "The 'Roof' Ghost of Waterbury," Famous Ghosts, *Brooklyn Daily Times*, October 3, 1922.
14. Carruth, "'Roof' Ghost of Waterbury."
15. Carruth, "'Roof' Ghost of Waterbury."
16. Carruth, "'Roof' Ghost of Waterbury."
17. Carruth, "'Roof' Ghost of Waterbury."
18. "A Haunted House," *Waterbury Daily American*, January 16, 1871.

19. As a matter of synchronicity, while the colonial specter was making his presence known in Waterbury's City Hall, Arthur Conan Doyle embarked on his North American lecture tour touting his startling views on Spiritualism. The series of discourses Doyle provided, from April 9 through June 24, 1922, are documented in *Our American Adventure* (George H. Doran Co., 1923). Here in Waterbury, the mystery writer's inaugural New York lecture is described in "Death Bed Sensations Told by Sir Arthur Conan Doyle," *Waterbury Republican*, April 13, 1922.
20. "City Hall Ghost Appears in Revolutionary Uniform," *Waterbury Republican*, April 15, 1922.
21. "City Hall Ghost Appears."
22. "City Hall Ghost Appears."
23. "City Hall Ghost Eludes Seven Subtle Sleuths—Mystery Unsolved," *Waterbury Republican*, April 19, 1922.
24. William J. Pape, *History of Waterbury and the Naugatuck Valley, Connecticut*, vol. 1 (S.J. Clarke Publishing, 1918), 21.
25. "City Hall Ghost Appears."
26. "Let the Ghost Walk," *Anaconda (MT) Standard*, April 23, 1922. Note: This newspaper's editorial staff expressed a warm kinship with the Naugatuck Valley due to Montana being a source for the raw material supporting Connecticut's brass industry.
27. "City Hall Ghost Appears."
28. Katherine A. Prichard, *Ancient Burying-Grounds of the Town of Waterbury, Connecticut* (Mattatuck Historical Society, 1917), 12.
29. "The Matter Well Under Way: The Old Grand Street Cemetery to Become City Property," *Waterbury Evening Democrat*, May 2, 1890.
30. "Library Park When It Was a Cemetery," *Waterbury Sunday Republican*, February 28, 1954.
31. John DiCorpo, "Park Forged Out of Bitterness, Claims of Desecration," *Sunday Republican* (Waterbury, CT), July 26, 1959.
32. "Matter Well Under Way."
33. "Wiping Out the Old Cemetery," *New Haven Register*, April 25, 1891.
34. "Waterbury's 'Black Friday,'" *Waterbury Daily Republican*, April 25, 1891.
35. "Removing the Headstones," *Waterbury Daily Republican*, April 25, 1891.
36. Prichard, *Ancient Burying-Grounds*.
37. Walter H. Holmes, MD, "The Condition of Bodies Long Buried," *Boston Medical and Surgical Journal*, July 23, 1891; "Wiping Out the Old Cemetery."
38. "Speaking of Taking Up the Bodies," *Waterbury Evening Democrat*, July 28, 1890.

39. Edward Thomas Turner (1835–1891), another one of Waterbury's entrepreneurs, deserves mention. His well-known home was located less than half a mile from the Naugatuck River and has a history of interesting residents. Turner was the wealthy proprietor of E.T. Turner & Co., one of the Naugatuck Valley's largest dry goods stores. His son, Charles E. Turner, was appointed U.S. consul general at Ottawa, Canada, by President William McKinley. Incredibly, while traveling through the Great White North to Boston in 1900, Charles survived a fall from a moving Canada Atlantic train. The Turner family's brush with miracles continued. In 1902, Charles's wife, Kate, saved the life of a Quebec game warden. While the wildlife official was being mauled by a black bear, Charles grabbed the warden's legs and Kate maneuvered behind the animal. She startled the bear and stopped the savage attack by grasping the bear's ear and twisting the animal's head ("Rescued From a Bear's Clutches by Consul General's Wife," *Wheeling [WV] Sunday Register*, December 7, 1902).
40. "Made Fortune But Not Friends; Rich Woman Kills Self," *World-News* (Roanoke, VA), December 29, 1926.
41. "News of Psychic Activities," *Occult Digest*, April 1927.
42. "Spinster's Suicide Is Traced to Loss of 'Phantom Lover,'" *Virginia-Pilot* (Norfolk, VA), December 23, 1926.
43. "Mystery Veils Strange Death of Woman Here," *Waterbury Republican*, December 22, 1926.
44. "Her Ghost Love Gone, Ends Life," *New York American*, December 23, 1926.
45. "Waterbury Spinster Kills Self with Gas," *Meriden Record*, December 23, 1926.
46. Lulu Morden's brave life and bold accomplishments deserve to be celebrated. Here are additional sources:

"Loss of Phantom Lover Believed to Have Caused Suicide," *Florida Times-Union*, December 23, 1926.

"Morden Funeral to Takes [*sic*] Place Today," *Waterbury Republican*, December 23, 1926.

Especially enlightening is this online article about Lulu Morden: Raechel Guest, "Morden Manufacturing," *Waterbury Thoughts*, January 3, 2014, https://waterburythoughts.blogspot.com (Guest provides an outstanding biography of Lulu Morden and examines the inventor's time in Waterbury).

Lulu Morden obituary notice, *Waterbury Republican*, December 23, 1926.

2. *House of Thorn and Echo: Rose Hill Cottage*

1. Alexander Dallas (1850–1939) was born in Forres, Scotland, and indeed served as the longtime groundskeeper at Rose Hill Cottage. He was also an extremely popular Waterbury florist. The gardener's death made front-page news, "Mr. Dallas cultivated many rare specimens and shrubbery and was considered one of the foremost floriculturists of the state," see "Local Florist Dies at Home," *Waterbury Democrat*, January 24, 1939. Articles in local newspapers around the time of his passing, as well as when the Dallas Flower Store closed, praised Alexander and happily reminisced about his celebrated shop. See "Son Assists at Father's Rites," *Waterbury Democrat*, January 26, 1939; "Long, Honorable Career," *Waterbury Democrat*, January 27, 1939; and "An Old Business Closes," *Waterbury Democrat*, December 12, 1942.
2. William Watkins, *Rose Hill: Its Architecture, Its History* (Mattatuck Museum, 1973) is located in Chase Family Papers, Box 11, Folder G, Max R. Traurig Library and Archive, Mattatuck Museum. For the architectural history of Waterbury's Hillside neighborhood, including Rose Hill Cottage, see Peter Haring Judd, *More Lasting Than Brass: A Thread of Family From Revolutionary New York to Industrial Connecticut* (Newbury Street Press & Northeastern University Press, 2004).
3. "The Haunted House at Waterbury," *Hartford Daily Courant*, October 1, 1884, states "[William Scovill's] wife being much addicted to strong drink."
4. Joseph Anderson, ed., *The Town and City of Waterbury, Connecticut, From the Aboriginal Period to the Year Eighteen Hundred and Ninety-Five*, vol. 2 (Price & Lee Company, 1896), 337. For a time, the Welton family resided at Brown's Hotel as shown in the 1860 United States Federal Census; a description of the hotel can be found in Anderson's *Town and City of Waterbury*; there is also a fine advertisement for Brown's Hotel in the 1871 *Waterbury City Directory*.
5. In his 1896 Waterbury history, Anderson notes in Mr. Welton's biography that the mill owner "So wholly absorbed was he in whatever he undertook, that neither heat nor cold nor food nor rest debarred him from attending to what his hand found to do. He was never known to take a vacation." Also, the booklet by William Watkins, *Rose Hill*, states, "Mr. Welton, obviously, was a man who was busy with the affairs of business and, apparently, found time for little else."
6. Mike Tedesco, interview by the author, May 27, 2022. While discussing nineteenth-century industrial Waterbury and America (on the front porch of Rose Hill Cottage), Mike Tedesco, senior director of operations

at the Greater Waterbury YMCA, shared the following encompassing visualization: "Come mornings old man Welton would wake up and head for the front door…" It is far too good a quote not to include in the story, and I thank Mike for letting me use the line.

7. "The Long Peak Victim," *New York Times*, September 28, 1884: "[Carrie Welton was a] striking-looking woman. She was finely educated and a brilliant horsewoman, with a propensity to do uncommon things and achieve a reputation for courage and physical endurance." Also, "Was Carrie J. Welton Insane?" *New Haven Evening Register*, November 30, 1884: "Welton was eccentric, strong-willed and very self-reliant."
8. Knight was discussed throughout the Welton family trial. See "About $150,000 Involved: The Welton Will Contest," *New Haven Evening Register*, October 14, 1886.
9. John P. Conway, "Jane Porter Welton of Rose Hill: A Mistress Who Matched Her Mansion," *Sunday Waterbury Republican Magazine*, March 30, 1969. According to the article, as late as 1969, Welton descendants were using this bowl for potato chips.
10. The theory that Carrie possibly murdered her father is detailed in Charles Monagan's fascinating novel, *Carrie Welton* (Penmore Press, 2016).
11. "About $150,000 Involved: The Welton Will Contest," *New Haven Evening Register*, October 14, 1886. Carrie Welton's excesses regarding Knight were brought to light during the trial in which the Welton family tried to negate Carrie's will on the grounds of insanity. See "Eccentric Miss Welton: Afraid of Being Poisoned," *New Haven Evening Register*, October 13, 1886. Knight either died in 1875, according to the article "$150,000 Involved: The Welton Will Contest," or Knight died in 1876 per the article "Eccentric Miss Welton: Afraid of Being Poisoned."
12. "Bequest to Bergh Contested: Report to Break the Will of Miss Caroline Welton, of, Waterbury," *New York Herald*, October 13, 1886.
13. Carrie's independent and demanding personality is evident here and certainly contributed to her fatal decision. See James H. Pickering, "Alone Amid the Wind's Mad Revelry: The Death of Carrie Welton," *Colorado Heritage Magazine*, Summer 1998, 5.
14. "Sketch of Carrie Welton," *St. Paul (MN) Daily Globe*, September, 29, 1884: "The opinion has become general that Miss Welton was deserted by the guide."
15. Janet Robertson, *The Magnificent Mountain Women: Adventures in the Colorado Rockies* (University of Nebraska Press, 2003).
16. Robertson, *Magnificent Mountain Women.*

17. James H. Pickering, "Alone Amid the Wind's Mad Revelry: The Death of Carrie Welton," *Colorado Heritage Magazine*, Summer 1998, 12. The quote first appeared in Elkanah Lamb's *Miscellaneous Meditations* (Publisher's Press Room and Bindery Company, [circa 1913]).
18. "Miss Welton's Wraith," *Leadville (CO) Daily Herald*, October 9, 1884, states, "There are a large number of people who firmly believe that the house is haunted." In another example of the house being commonly accepted as the scene of preternatural activity, the article "Carrie J. Welton's Will," *New Haven Evening Register*, December 23, 1884, explains that when a subpoena was served to Jane Welton after Carrie's death, "no officer could gain admission to her house, the *haunted* Rose Hill Cottage" (emphasis added). Also, "State News," *New Haven Morning Journal and Courier*, June 7, 1886 reiterates, "The place is one of the finest hereabouts, but some will insist that the place has been haunted by Miss Welton's spirit ever since her death."
19. "The Haunted House of Waterbury," *Hartford Daily Courant*, October 1, 1884; "A Haunted Mansion," *Kansas City Times*, October 7, 1884.
20. "A Haunted Mansion," *Biddeford (ME) Daily Journal*, October 1, 1884: "But now the place is looked upon with a sort of fear, and people instinctively shudder as they pass [Rose Hill Cottage], dreading to look up into the groves and lawns through fear of seeing some spirits of evil." Also, "Woes of the Weltons: Miss Carrie, the Mountain Climber—The Haunted Mansion," *Kansas City Star*, October 1, 1884: "People pass by the great Welton mansion with a shudder." And in, "The Haunted House at Waterbury," *Hartford Daily Courant*, October 1, 1884: "Although the property was put in the market at a low figure, it is impossible to sell it, as it is firmly believed that a curse rests upon it."
21. "A Haunted Mansion," *Kansas City Times*, October 7, 1884: "All sorts of stories are in circulation today about the old mansion, one of which was that the [deceased] daughter had been seen in the yard on horseback at midnight."
22. "Is This House Haunted? A Ghastly Waterbury Tale," *New Haven Evening Register*, September 30, 1884, mysteriously intones, "Several families have attempted to reside there since the Weltons left, but soon gave it up, although not publicly assigning any reasons therefor."
23. "Mrs. Martha Proper of Holabird, Hyde County, Dak.," *New Haven Morning Journal and Courier*, September 12, 1887, states: "[Martha Proper] has heard that the Welton estate here is haunted and for sale and writes to Postmaster Commerford for the price. Rose Hill Cottage, she may be

told, is not haunted enough to make it interesting for a Dakota woman." In the end, Proper never purchased the mansion.

24. An excellent history of Waterbury's romantic landmark can be found in Raechel Guest, "Welton Horse Fountain," *Waterbury Thoughts*, November 26, 2016, http://waterburythoughts.blogspot.com/.
25. "The Welton Case," *New Haven Morning Journal and Courier*, October 26, 1886: "Alexander Dallas a florist, who sometimes had the care of the grounds around Rose Hill Cottage, said he never saw anything in Carrie's actions, language or appearance which might give the opinion that she was insane."

3. Who Knocks?

1. "Died," *The Derby Transcript*, February 17, 1886; "Ansonia," *New Haven Evening Register*, February 15, 1886.
2. "The Great Rain," *The Derby Transcript*, February 17, 1886, noted, "The heaviest rain for several years" ended on Saturday, February 13, the identical day as Miss Ryan's passing. This same newspaper reported under an "Ansonia" dateline that "Main Street mud has been something to remark upon the past few days."
3. The superstition surrounding the removal of knots and pins from a corpse is detailed in "A Strange Proceeding," *New Haven Evening Register*, February 18, 1886.
4. "Strange Proceeding." The surreal cemetery activity was also discussed at length in "Sensations in a Cemetery," *New York Herald*, February 19, 1886, and the *Seymour Record*, February 26, 1886, briefly reported on the Ansonia cemetery folk-belief commotion but claimed it was merely a rumor.
5. "Sensations in a Cemetery."
6. "Strange Proceeding." Note: Tales surrounding the Ansonia disinterment appeared in contemporary newspapers across the country. However, the actual name of the poor woman whose grave was reopened remained a mystery for nearly a century and a half. The identity, and ordeal, of Miss Jeannie Ryan is acknowledged for the first time here in *Haunted Waterbury & the Naugatuck Valley*. Drawing from contemporary Ansonia, Connecticut death notices, which coincide with newspaper coverage of the cemetery visit and the subsequent pin's removal (on February 17, 1886) and then linking an Irish surname and gender to the deceased deductively lead to Miss Ryan as the most likely candidate. Her Christian name appeared

in death notices using various spellings, alternatively printed as Jeannie, Jennie and Jeanne. This story employs "Jeannie," as it is the name listed in the local *Derby Transcript* obituary column titled, "Died."

4. The Midnight Watchman

1. One of the largest, and oldest, of the Naugatuck Valley's brass concerns, the forges of Wallace & Son's cast an important glow across America's burgeoning industrial revolution. Nestled in Ansonia adjacent to the river, the brass and copper mill's scattered assortment of gargantuan buildings resembled the toppled constructs of some lost Cyclopean civilization. According to the *Illustrated Review of the Naugatuck Valley*, the company commenced operations in 1848 and two years later relocated to the larger area near downtown. Within forty years' time, Wallace's employed seven hundred specialized laborers within its rolling mills, wire mills and ancillary facilities.

   Today these abandoned brick husks are a silent memorial to an era when the Valley's manufacturers dominated the world's brass industry. The significant role that this golden-hued metal attained during the decades of America's Industrial Age cannot be underappreciated. Ubiquitous brass was crafted into every item imaginable. From jacket buttons to tea kettles, train whistles, bullet cartridges and rooftops, there was nary an object not made of brass. The *New York Times* defined this alloy as the nineteenth century's equivalent of today's plastic. Brass was the malleable currency of Victorian industrialists, and for more than a century, the globe's proverbial Fort Knox of brass was located in and around Ansonia, up and down the Naugatuck River.
2. *Illustrated Review of the Naugatuck Valley* (Sovereign Publishing and Engraving Company, 1891), 23. The smokestack was constructed in 1875 using half a million bricks; at eight feet wide, the clockface was easily visible across the river.
3. "Emil Fritz's Ghost: A Mysterious Occurrence Which Astonished a Watchman at Wallace & Sons," *New Haven Register*, June 10, 1886.
4. "State and Vicinity," "Emil Fritz of Ansonia," *Seymour Record*, February 26, 1886; "The Funeral of Emil Fritz," *New Haven Register*, February 22, 1886.
5. Mrs. Caroline Fritz was born in the state of Georgia. The children's names are gleaned from Ancestry.com, 1880 United States Federal Census: Place: Derby, New Haven, Connecticut; Roll: 104; Page: 183B. The unnamed

toddler was born well after the 1880 Census. The family's home address is identified by consulting, "Fritz, Emil," in the *Derby, Shelton and Seymour Directory 1886–7* (Price, Lee & Co., 1886), 73.
6. "Emil Fritz's Ghost."
7. Details of the shooting as related by Mrs. Fritz and daughter Gertrude appear in "Suicide in Ansonia," *Derby Transcript*, February 24, 1886; a slightly different account appears in "With a Revolver: Emil Fritz, An Ansonia Man, Ends His Life With a Pistol Shot Yesterday Afternoon," *Morning Journal and Courier* (New Haven, CT), February 20, 1886.
8. "Suicide in Ansonia."
9. Emil's friendship with Dr. Welch is noted in "The Emil Fritz Mystery," *New Haven Register*, March 1, 1886. Welch was fondly thought of as one of New England's last "old time family physician[s]" in the biography "William Collin Welch, M.D. New Haven," *Proceedings of the Connecticut State Medical Society 1925* (Published by the Society, 1925).
10. "State News," *New Haven Register*, February 26, 1886.
11. Dr. Beardsley's biographical information is from Samuel Orcutt, "George Lucius Beardsley, M.D.," *The History of the Old Town of Derby, Connecticut* (Press of the Springfield Printing Company, 1880), 531–32; J.L. Rockey, ed., *History of New Haven County, Connecticut*, vol. 2 (W.W. Preston & Co., 1892), 440–41.
12. "It Now Transpires," *Derby Transcript*, February 24, 1886; "The Emil Suicides: Two Bullets. One of Them Intended for His Wife—Jealousy the Cause," *New Haven Register*, February 23, 1886; "Emil Fritz Mystery."
13. "Emil Fritz Mystery."
14. "Connecticut: A Day's Sensation in a Sensational State," *Springfield (MA) Republican*, March 2, 1886.
15. "Emil Fritz Mystery"; "Connecticut: A Day's Sensation."
16. Emil's "passionate and excitable nature," is noted in "Suicide in Ansonia."
17. "A Murder Mystery: Strange Circumstances Connected with the Death of a Connecticut Man," *Plain Dealer* (Cleveland, OH), March 1, 1886.
18. See the listing for "Dover, Robert A., Watchman W. & Sons, h[ouse] 7 Winter, A[sonia]," in *Ansonia, Birmingham, Derby, Shelton and Seymour Directory, 1887–8*.
19. "Carrie Frits [Fritz]" married John N. Cors Jr., Ancestry.com, New York, New York, U.S., Extracted Marriage Index, 1866–1937.
20. "Cors" obituary, *Brooklyn Daily Eagle*, October 11, 1928.
21. "March 7, 1917—Old Wallace Stack Is Being Torn Down," Derby Historical Society, https://www.derbyhistorical.org.

5. Tales of the Bloody Hookman

1. There is a ghastly and lengthy list of Hookman origin tales. Background stories about the Hookman and how he met (or didn't meet) his end can be found online. Recounting a few of these sources includes Katherine Ripley, "Creepy Backstories and Versions of the Hook Man Legend," *Graveyard Shift*, September 23, 2021, https://www.ranker.com (Ripley's article highlights five bloody scenarios concerning the Hookman and his victims as well as a brief discussion about the legend's moral); "Hookman's Ghost, Seymour, Connecticut," *Illuminating Shadows: Dark Folklore, Strange History and Morbid Curiosities*, April 27, 2013, http://illuminating-shadows.blogspot.com/2013; David Mikkelson, "The Hook: An Escaped Killer Interrupts a Young Couple's Make-Out Session," *Snopes*, December 2, 1998. https://www.snopes.com.
2. Hookman stories have long swirled around the Seymour cemetery, see "Hookman's Cemetery, Seymour (Great Hill Cemetery)," *Damned Connecticut*, https://www.damnedct.com; Robin Reeve, "Haunted Hookman's Cemetery-Seymour, CT," *Ghostwatcherz*, February 20, 2011, http://www.ghostwatcherz.com/.
3. Prudence Mackintosh, "Texarkana Murder Mystery," *Texas Monthly* 42, no. 12 (December 2014): 37–40.
4. "'Sundown' Is Thumbs Down in Every Way," *Schenectady (NY) Gazette*, March 12, 1977. Dan DiNicola's review of the film includes the oft-retold Hookman legend, "Back in college in the early '60s, everyone claimed he had a friend who, while parking with a girl, heard a radio flash about an escaped lunatic with an artificial, hooked hand. As the story goes, the girl says, 'let's get out of here.' They take off, but once safe in his date's driveway, the boy goes to open her door and there dangling from the handle is a hook. The kids in 'Sundown' aren't so lucky."
5. Carolyn DeLieto, interview by the author regarding Hookman legends and Great Hill Cemetery, January 21, 2023, and May 19, 2023.
6. Tony Perry, "Stories That Shaped the Century, From the Pages of the Los Angeles Times; Effects of Chessman's Execution in 1960," *Los Angeles Times*, November 12, 1999.
7. Abigail Van Buren, "Dear Abby," nationally syndicated newspaper column, November 8, 1960.
8. Regarding cautionary motifs, folklorist Dr. Faye Ringel (professor emerita of humanities, U.S. Coast Guard Academy) discusses "Hookman's Cemetery" and various teenage-behavioral deterrent legends during her

WPLR 99.1FM interview, which aired on the *Chaz & AJ in the Morning* show's annual *Freak Week* program, October 27, 2022.

9. Perhaps the best examination of the Hookman appears in Jan Harold Brunvand, *The Vanishing Hitchhiker: American Urban Legends & Their Meaning* (W.W. Norton, 1981), 48–52. Brunvand includes a dynamic discussion about the sociological impact of this urban legend. The work also lists the states where the Hookman mythos has circulated. For an excellent examination of the Hookman's New Jersey incarnations, consult Kathleen Andrysiak-Goff, "The Hookman of Runyon," *New Jersey Folklore* 10 (1985): 30–34. The Hookman terrorizing Mulholland Drive above Los Angeles is mentioned in Patricia Ward Biederman, "Folklorist's College Archive Collects Clues to Who We Are; Legends: Trove of Folk Wisdom and Tales Ranging from the Hook Man to Cures for Warts Offers Insights Into Behavior," *Los Angeles Times*, February 27, 2000, B5.
10. Aly Butler, interview by the author conducted at the Valley Diner, Derby, Connecticut, on January 21, 2023, regarding Great Hill's haunted wilderness.
11. Donna Jacobson, "The Hookman of Montville," *Montville Patch*, August 7, 2011.

6. Occurrences in the Birmingham National Bank: A Tale of Two Vaults

1. Michael Picone (Twisted Vine Restaurant owner), interview by the author, August 30, 2024, and September 3, 2024.
2. Charles Gillespie, *Souvenir History of Derby and Shelton, Connecticut* (Transcript Co., 1896), 27–29.
3. John R. Fogerty, interview by the author throughout April 2024 and August 25, 2024.
4. Nicholas Howard, interview by the author, April 20, 2024.
5. Michael Picone and David Harmon (Twisted Vine's head waiter), interview by the author, April 11, 2024.
6. David Harmon, interview by the author, April 11, 2024, and September 3, 2024.
7. Jean Falbo-Sosnovich, "Ghost Hunters to Spend the Night at Derby's 'Haunted' Twisted Vine," *New Haven Register*, February 18, 2019.
8. Amy Bruni, *Food to Die For* (Harper Celebrate, 2024), 125.
9. Liliana Feliciano (Twisted Vine Restaurant staff), interview by the author, August 30, 2024, and September 1, 2024. All quotes regarding Liliana

Feliciano's paranormal experiences were gathered during the author's interviews conducted with Ms. Feliciano on August 30, 2024, at the Twisted Vine Restaurant and on September 1, 2024, at Derby's Valley Diner.

10. Feliciano, interview by author, September 1, 2024.
11. "Derby Banker Shot Himself," *Meriden Record Journal*, November 18, 1913.
12. "S.H. Lessey Suicides," *Daily Advocate* (Stamford, CT), November 18, 1913.
13. *Ansonia, Derby, Shelton and Seymour Directory 1913* (Price & Lee Co., 1913), 477.
14. "Shelton: Hearings on the Buckingham Will Matter," *Newtown Bee*, December 31, 1897.
15. "Rufus W. Blake Dead," *New York Tribune*, October 27, 1901.
16. "Rich Man May Be Fatally Shot," *New York Tribune*, October 19, 1901.
17. Additional sources (beyond those appearing in these endnotes) regarding the fascinating Mr. Lessey's steadfast life and sad demise include: "Bank Cashier Ends His Life," *Norwich Morning News*, November 18, 1913; "Check Raising Not Cause of Suicide," *The Day* (New London, CT), November 18, 1913; "He Kills Himself at Tomb," *New Haven Union*, November 18, 1913; "Suicide Cashier's Accounts Correct," *Springfield (MA) Union*, November 18, 1913; "Suicide of Bank Cashier Caused by Steeve's Sins," *Bridgeport Evening Farmer*, November 18, 1913.

7. Inside the Naugatuck Valley Vortex: Strange Sights Overhead

1. Dr. J. Allen Hynek, *Night Siege: The Hudson Valley UFO Sightings* (Llewellyn Publications, 1998), 5.
2. "A Large Tree Burned by Lightning," *Morning Journal and Courier* (New Haven, CT), August 7, 1888.
3. "Saturday's Storm," *Waterbury Daily American*, August 6, 1888.
4. "Saturday's Storm."
5. "A Ball of Fire at Long Lake—Remarkable Phenomenon," *Morning Journal and Courier* (New Haven, CT), August 7, 1888.
6. "Ball of Fire at Long Lake."
7. Letter to the Editor, *Waterbury Daily American*, August 6, 1892.
8. "—That Someone Sends Up a Big Fire Balloon…," *Waterbury Daily American*, August 8, 1892.
9. "Strange Aircraft Over Scovill Plant," *Hartford Courant*, March 10, 1916.
10. "Mysterious Aircraft Visits Scovill's…Appears Above Plant Near Midnight; Guards Thrown Into Turmoil," *Waterbury Republican*, March 10, 1916.

11. "Mysterious Aircraft Visits Scovill's."
12. "Airship Alarms Waterbury," *The Daily Advocate* (Stamford, CT), March 10, 1916.
13. "Strange Aircraft Over Scovill Plant."
14. "Aircraft Again Reported Seen Above the City," *Waterbury Republican*, March 11, 1916.
15. "Mysterious Airship Over Scoville [*sic*] Plant, Waterbury," *Norwich Bulletin*, March 10, 1916.
16. "Airship Alarms Waterbury."
17. "Mysterious Aircraft Visit's Scovill's."
18. "Aircraft Again Reported Seen."
19. "Aircraft Again Reported Seen."
20. Adam Janos, "Why Have There Been So Many UFO Sightings Near Nuclear Facilities?," *HISTORY*, June 23, 2019, https://www.history.com.
21. "Mysterious Aircraft Visits Scovill's."

8. The Kinneytown Entity

1. Reverend Hollis Campbell and William C. Sharpe, *Seymour, Past and Present* (W.C. Sharpe, 1902). A valuable source, this work describes the evolution of the town as well as its appearance at the turn of the last century. Frank G. Bassett authored the Genealogy History of Seymour section which includes the local Kenney family tree.
2. Campbell and Sharpe, *Seymour, Past and Present*, 19.
3. "A Kinneytown Ghost," *Ansonia Evening Sentinel*, November 18, 1896.
4. "A Novel Nutmeg Ghost," *The Sun* (New York, NY), November 29, 1896.
5. John Matthews and Caitlin Matthews, *The Element Encyclopedia of Magical Creatures* (Barnes & Noble, 2008), 393. In the section titled, "Road Predators," John and Caitlin Matthews explain, "These haunters of the lonely road are often location-specific, patrolling a particular road or region....In many cases, it is what is not seen but felt that causes the traveler alarm." Also, see John Geiger, *The Third Man Factor* (Weinstein Books, 2009), 14. Geiger explains that he haunted road phenomena mimics "Third Man" manifestations, though in the Kinneytown case, it looms as an evil entity. Regarding "Third Man" situations, "Over the years, the experience has occurred again and again, not only to 9/11 survivors, mountaineers, and divers, but also to polar explorers, prisoners of war, solo sailors, shipwreck survivors, aviators, and astronauts....This

presence offered a sense of protection, relief, guidance, and hope, and left the person convinced he or she was not alone but that there was some other being at his or her side, when by any normal calculation there was none." This benevolent presence can be shadowy or solid, young or old, male or female, and is intent upon accompanying and protecting the group or individual. The phrase "Third Man" originates in T.S. Eliot's commentary on the heroic Shackleton expedition and appears in his poem *The Waste Land* (Horace Liveright, 1922), 43: "Who is the third who walks always beside you? When I count, there are only you and I together. But when I look ahead up the white road, There is always another one walking beside you."

6. "Novel Nutmeg Ghost."
7. "Novel Nutmeg Ghost."
8. "Teamsters Found Guilty," *New Haven Evening Register*, July 11, 1903; "The Trolley to Derby," *Daily Morning Journal and Courier* (New Haven, CT), February 9, 1903. Minott Arthur Smith's (1862–1943) ancestral farm rested on the land bordering Derby and Orange, Connecticut, on what was known during Smith's time as both the Derby Turnpike and New Haven Road (near Willow, now Willard Road). Today, this thoroughfare (Derby Avenue) is commonly referred to as Route 34. His farmhouse was located about half a mile west of the Sodom Lane–Grassy Hill Road intersection. As for family, Minott came from staunch Yankee lineage. His father was a constable. His grandfather was a farmer and selectmen. When Minott Smith married Grace Nichols in 1891, he sought secure financial means to support his new family. Newlyweds Grace and Minott relocated near the Canadian border, where Minott worked for an Adirondack lumber company (they would return to Connecticut after just a few years due to Grace's illness). Back on the family farm, Minott took his place as a respected member of the local community. In 1898, Minott's 2,600-plus-pound draft horse team won second place at the inaugural Orange Grange Fair. Neither backbreaking work nor burly backwoods roughnecks intimidated Minott Smith. Once, while delivering a four-horse rig for repair in the Westville section of New Haven, Smith found himself in the midst of a labor strike. Waggoneers like Minott Smith were confronted in the Elm City by roving roadblocks and threatened with bodily injury. Minott boldly announced to the angry workers, "If you'll mind your own business, I'll mind mine," and calmly proceeded forward. Later that day, the same agitators pursued Minott down Water Street and pelted the farmer with

a barrage of stones. Minott owned extensive property on the Derby-Orange line. The extent of his holdings can be accurately judged when considering that just one of his barns was lent out to the Connecticut Railway & Lighting Company to house eighty laborers constructing the local trolley line during 1903. Later in life, Smith was employed by the railroad. He married twice, first to Grace Nichols Smith (1874–1894) of the Deerfield section of Newtown. Grace died of consumption; she was just nineteen years old. Minott's second wife was Georgianna Roberts Smith (1879–1925). During the later years of the World Depression, Minott Smith served his community as a selectman for the town of Orange (1936–1941). The Freemason was an imposing New Englander.

9. "A Kinneytown Ghost," *Waterbury Democrat*, November 18, 1896.
10. "Novel Nutmeg Ghost."
11. "At a Late Hour," *The Seymour Record*, November 19, 1896.
12. The weird encounter between this monstrous creature and the two Seymour men is brought to light in "Local Briefs," *The Seymour Record*, November 14, 1901. The newspaper's sparse account reads more like the coverage of a strange event that might appear in H.P. Lovecraft's fictional newspaper, *Arkham Advertiser*.
13. There is an excellent paranormal saving grace for those of us living on the shores of the Naugatuck River, and indeed all rivers, concerning the long folkloric tradition of supernatural creatures being unable to traverse running water. "The popular idea that spirits cannot cross running water may have arisen from the primitive belief as to the river-crossing that the deceased has to [inevitably] encounter [as they pass from this world and into the next…as in the case of the River Styx; once crossed, the departed can never return]. A familiar application of this notion will occur to the reader in the legend of 'Tam o' Shanter.' It will be remembered that as soon as Tam has reached the 'key-stance o' the brig' he is beyond the pursuit of the witches. 'A running stream they darena [*sic*] cross,'" according to Marion Roalfe Cox in *An Introduction to Folk-Lore* (Charles Scribner's Sons, 1895), 185–86.
14. There are other variants on this theme concerning spirits being unable to negotiate running water. The online source *Occult World: Making the Invisible Visible* (https://occult-world.com) notes, "Crossing running water is a remedy against supernatural entities. According to widespread folklore beliefs, water is pure and holy and will reject the unholy. A person threatened or pursued by ghosts, fairies, demons, witches, vampires, and so forth can halt them in their tracks by crossing running water." (Note to self: for those

living on the Naugatuck River, this could be a helpful paranormal survival tactic). This concept is reinforced by Miriam Reid, who, expounding on the purity of water in mythology and science, notes, "The protective power of running water recurs in stories about vampires, ghosts, and other strange and mythical creatures." See Reid's article "River Gods, Lake Monsters, and the Abiding Power of Myth," *Distillations Magazine: Unexpected Stories from Science's Past*, February 1, 2022. Americans are readily familiar with the folklore of rivers/river crossings being able to repel monsters; consider Washington Irving's Headless Horseman halting his pursuit of Icabod Crane when the demon approaches the Sleepy Hollow Bridge ("The Legend of Sleepy Hollow," 1820).

9. Seymour's Empty Sepulcher Sings a Silent Chantey

1. Because no body is buried here, the memorial marker is known as a cenotaph. It's Joseph D. Wooster's identification that provides the main clue in determining the stone's missing name, which is his father, Ephraim. *Connecticut, U.S., Hale Collection of Cemetery Inscriptions and Newspaper Notices, 1629–1934*, ancestry.com, and Find A Grave, https://www.findagrave.com/. The cenotaph's inscription includes the date and location of Ephraim's death, thus confirming the fact.
2. Records conflict as to what rank and whether the Ephraim Wooster depicted in this story participated in the Revolutionary War. See *Lineage Book: National Society of the Daughters of the American Revolution*, vol. 24, *1898*. Also, Mary Philotheta Root, *Chapter Sketches: Connecticut Daughters of the American Revolution: Patriot's Daughters* (Connecticut Chapter DAR, 1904). The latter work attributes military records of a Huntington, Connecticut resident, Ephraim Wooster (1755–1838), and employs them inaccurately with the military dossier of Waterbury, Connecticut-born Ephraim Wooster (1764–1830), who was on board the steamboat *United States*.
3. Ephraim's service as a tax collector is mentioned in, "Notice Is Hereby Given," *Connecticut Journal* (New Haven, CT), November 14, 1805.
4. As for Beecher's innovation of steamboat tickets and a good description of the captain's character, see Roger Williams McAdam, *Salts of the Sound: An Informal History of Steamboat Days and the Famous Skippers Who Sailed Long Island Sound* (Stephen Daye Press, 1957), 32–34. Further note: Upon retiring in 1833, after years of commanding Long Island Sound sailing packets and steamboats, Beecher as a member of the Whig Party served

nearly two decades as New Haven's first selectman. He died in 1858, at the age of eighty-three, a remarkable and well-respected man.

5. For information about the construction and history of the steamship *United States*, see Fred Erving Dayton, *Steamboat Days* (Frederick A. Stokes Company, 1925); Samuel Ward Stanton, *American Steam Vessels* (Smith & Stanton, 1895). Regarding the fate of the steamboat *United States*, it left Long Island Sound in 1832 to once again shuttle the Hudson River. Eight years later, the *United States* was removed from service and broken up.
6. An interesting history of the New Haven Steamboat Company's founding is provided in *Annual Book, City of New Haven, No. 11: Containing Lists of the Officers of City Government, Messages of the Mayor, Reports and Other Public Documents, for 1871–1872* (Tuttle, Morehouse & Taylor, 1872).
7. Beecher's coarse mannerisms were legendary. When the captain retired in 1833, a Massachusetts newspaper noted, "[Beecher] was the most uncomfortable [travel] companion, and the most uncivil, surly fellow that ever had control of a steamboat," *Boston Traveler*, May 7, 1833. News of his death in 1858 prompted the editor of a Hartford, Connecticut newspaper to soften Captain Beecher's use of colorful language: "He was a rough burly man, with a warm heart under a surly exterior....In moments of excitement, [Beecher] used to be *slightly* profane [emphasis added]," *Connecticut Courant* (Hartford, CT), January 16, 1858.
8. "Beecher's suspended chicken coop" is humorously mentioned in Dayton, *Steamboat Days*.
9. "Lunatics, Inmates, and Homeowners: The History of Roosevelt Island," Museum of the City of New York, https://blog.mcny.org. "After New York City gained ownership of [Blackwell's] island in 1828, construction began on a series of public institutions, including a prison, an almshouse, and several hospitals."
10. "Before Rikers: Blackwell's Was DOC's Island Home, Part 1 of 3," special issue of *Correction News* marking DOC's centennial, 1995. "The facilities the city constructed on Blackwell's—the Charity Hospital, Penitentiary, Alms House, Hospital for Incurables, Workhouse, Asylum for the Insane, among others—were built of granite in the fortress style from feudal times."
11. Details of the steamboat disaster, often conflicting in nature, are re-created as accurately as possible through contemporary newspaper accounts. All newspapers date from September 1830: *Alexandria (VA) Gazette*, *American Mercury* (Hartford, CT), *Columbian Register* (New Haven), *Commercial Advisor*

(New York), *Connecticut Gazette* (New London, CT), *Evening Post* (New York), *The Farmer's Cabinet* (Amherst, NH), *Litchfield (CT) Enquirer*, *New-York American for the Country* (New York), *New-York Observer* (New York), *Norwich (CT) Republican* and *Spectator* (New York).

12. Martin Wells's ordeal aboard the *United States* is noted in the *New York Evening Post*, Wednesday, September 15, 1830. Martin's brief hospitalization in the almshouse is documented in "Almshouse Ledgers, 1758–1952," Ancestry, https://www.ancestry.com. Mr. Wells having been moved to Bellevue Hospital is noted in several newspaper accounts.

13. Harvey O. Shelley survived his steamship ordeal and eventually returned to sea, signing onboard the whaleship *Connecticut* in June 1831: Mystic Seaport Museum Library, *New London Crew Lists, 1803–1878*. It wasn't until Harvey returned from hunting whales in the South Atlantic in early 1832 that he learned that his brother, Joel Ward Shelley, had died at sea on November 22, 1831. Harvey later married Lois Dowd in 1834. He passed away on December 29, 1855.

14. *Minutes of the Common Council of the City of New York, 1784–1831*, vol. 16, *January 2, 1827 to February 25, 1828* (Published by the City of New York, 1917). Woodruff was appointed keeper of the penitentiary on March 26, 1827.

15. A shocking description of Ephraim's body is detailed in "Melancholy Steamboat Accident," *Alexandria (VA) Gazette*, September 17, 1830.

16. Even Seymour, Connecticut's erudite historian W.C. Sharpe in his "Inscriptions in Great Hill Cemetery," mistakenly labels the placename as "the Island of *Betize*," in W.C. Sharpe, *Vital Statistics of Seymour, Conn.* (Record Print, 1883), 95.

17. *History and Description of the Now Lost City of Balize, Louisiana, from 1921* (Louisiana Works Progress, 1921), 2. Originally appeared in Meigs O. Foster, *New Orleans Item*, October 9, 1921, https://louisianadigitallibrary.org. "Swift and riotous life, sudden and violent death, wild men and wilder women, red liquor, keen-edged knife and crashing pistol, all night orgies that ended with a string of murders at dawn—these were the scenes enacted where now the Lone Tomb rises."

18. Treasure hunting activity is documented in *History and Description of the Now Lost City of Balize*, 3.

10. Something Wicked Slithers in Purgatory: The Watertown Wyrm

1. Marguerite Allis, *Connecticut Trilogy* (G.P. Putnam's Sons, 1934), 209.
2. "The Serpent in the Stone: Is 'Dragon' Rock a Work of Art or a Freak of Nature?," *Sunday Republican* (Waterbury, CT), May 16, 2010.
3. "A Nova Scotia Hill Snake Story," *Waterbury Daily American*, July 22, 1892.
4. "Nova Scotia Hill Snake Story."
5. "Nova Scotia Hill Snake Story."
6. "Nova Scotia Hill Snake Story."
7. "Nova Scotia Hill Snake Story."
8. "Fools Not All Dead Yet—But Who's the Fool?," *Waterbury Daily American*, August 8, 1892.
9. "In Watertown: A Brand New Snake Story—A Monster Reported Seen in Curtis Dayton's Swamp," *Morning Journal and Courier* (New Haven, CT), September 16, 1896.
10. "The Watertown Snake," *The Hartford Courant*, May 28, 1895.
11. "A Snake Story," *New Haven Register*, May 28, 1895.
12. "In Watertown."
13. "In Watertown."
14. "In Watertown."
15. "In Watertown."
16. "In Watertown."
17. "In Watertown."
18. "The Connecticut Man Who Saw a Monster Serpent," *Riverside (CA) Daily Press*, October 16, 1896.
19. "Seth Bassett's Vision," *Erie (PA) Times-News*, September 19, 1896.
20. "That Watertown Snake: Old Reptile 'Seen Again,' This Time by a Tramp," *Waterbury Daily American*, August 12, 1899.
21. "That Watertown Snake."
22. "That Watertown Snake."
23. "That Watertown Snake."
24. "Watertown's Snake: Like Other Things in the Valley It Is a Big One," *Ansonia Evening Sentinel*, July 28, 1900.
25. "Large Snake Crawls into a House and Attacks a Rug," *Waterbury Evening Democrat*, June 17, 1902.
26. "Snakes in Connecticut," *Waterbury Daily American*, July 25, 1892.
27. "A Monster Snake Seen," *Waterbury Evening Democrat*, July 22, 1895.
28. "Circus Forgot A 'Worm,'" *Norwalk Hour*, July 22, 1912.

29. "Room Full of Snakes: Express Company Officials Receive a Scare," *Wilkes-Barre (PA) Times*, September 27, 1906.
30. "Social Life Stops While Town Hunts for Python," *New Britain Herald*, July 18, 1930.
31. "To the Editor of the American," *Waterbury Daily American*, August 14, 1899.
32. The following sources were also consulted when preparing the Watertown Wyrm chapter: Florence T. Crowell's *Historic Watertown, Connecticut Photo Gallery*, originally posted on July 17, 2019, includes, "Rattlesnake on the Prowl in Watertown," unidentified newspaper source, dated July 27, 1894, accessed July 22, 2021. Currently posted online as *Watertown History Page by Charlie Crowell*, https://www.facebook.com/334846928460/posts/rattlesnake-on-the-prowl-in-watertownwatertown-conn-july-27-1894-a-large-rattles/10156382305963461; Tim MacSweeney, "Serpent Thoughts (Without Feathers)," *Waking Up On Turtle Island: Indigenous Ceremonial Stone Landscapes of Turtle Island*, May 23, 2010, accessed August 10, 2021. http://wakinguponturtleisland.blogspot.com/2010/05/serpent-thoughts-with-out-feathers.html; Clifford B. Moore, "America's Mythical Snakes," *The Scientific Monthly*, January 1949; Joseph Anderson, ed., *The Town and City of Waterbury, Connecticut From the Aboriginal Period to the Year Eighteen Hundred and Ninety-Five*, vols. 1 and 3 (Price & Lee Company, 1896); "River History," The Quinnipiac River Fund website, accessed October 2, 2021, https://the quinnipiacriver.com/about/river-history; Diane Ciba (curator, Watertown History Museum), interview by the author concerning the Watertown, Connecticut name origins of Nova Scotia Hill and Purgatory, October 5, 2021; *Taylor's Souvenir of the Capitol, 1897–1898…of the State of Connecticut* (William Harrison Taylor, 1897) presents a very good contemporary biography of Judge George Cowell. The following newspapers were also consulted: *Ansonia Evening Sentinel* (1897) and *Evening Sentinel* (Ansonia, CT) (1900); *Boston Herald* (1892); *Hartford Courant* (1892, 1895); *Morning News* (Savannah, GA) (1899); *New Haven Journal and Courier* (1892, 1896); *New Haven Daily Morning Journal and Courier* (1906); *New Haven Register* (1895, 1900); *Repository* (Canton, OH) (1896); *Waterbury Daily American* (1892); *Waterbury Daily Republican* (1886); *Waterbury Evening Democrat* (1902).

11. The Devil's Address

1. "Fires in Seymour," *Columbian Weekly Register* (New Haven, CT), June 9, 1866; "The Great Hill Wild Man," *Evening Sentinel* (Ansonia, CT), March 8, 1899. Examples of strange stories taking place on Great Hill include a rash of unexplained fires and a wild man who believed he was possessed by devils.
2. "Great Is Great Hill," *The Derby Transcript*, July 22, 1885.
3. "Fritz Dame of Great Hill," *Morning Journal and Courier* (New Haven, CT), April 3, 1899.
4. "Curious Case," *Derby Journal*, November 21, 1850.
5. Reverend Hollis Andrew Campbell, William C. Sharpe and Frank G. Bassett, *Seymour, Past and Present* (W.C. Sharpe, 1902), 110, 117.
6. Campbell, Sharpe and Bassett, *Seymour, Past and Present*, 116–17; "Origin of 'Hell Lane,'" *Evening Sentinel* (Ansonia, CT), August 8, 1902.
7. Norman Litchfield, *A History of Christ Church, Quaker Farms in Oxford, Connecticut* (Edwards Brothers, Inc., 1954), 6–7.
8. "A Curious Case."
9. "Origin of 'Hell Lane,'" *Evening Sentinel* (Ansonia, CT), August 8, 1902.
10. "'Hell Lane' Again," *The Seymour Record*, August 7, 1902; "Origin of 'Hell Lane.'"
11. Campbell, Sharpe and Bassett, *Seymour, Past and Present*, 110.
12. "The Old Hotel," *The Seymour Record*, September 4, 1902.
13. Campbell, Sharpe and Bassett, *Seymour, Past and Present*, 117.
14. Campbell, Sharpe and Bassett, *Seymour, Past and Present*, 110.
15. Samuel Orcutt and Ambrose Beardsley, *The History of the Old Town of Derby, Connecticut, 1642–1880* (Press of Springfield Printing Company, 1880), 206; "Page from Derby's History: The First Bell and the Discord It Aroused," *Evening Sentinel* (Ansonia, CT), January 19, 1900.
16. Campbell, Sharpe and Bassett, *Seymour, Past and Present*, 110.
17. "Hell Lane and Rogues Alley," *The Seymour Record*, August 21, 1902.
18. Campbell, Sharpe and Bassett, *Seymour, Past and Present*, 119.
19. Campbell, Sharpe and Bassett, *Seymour, Past and Present*, 119.
20. Michael Bielawa, "The Night of the Wakemanite Ritual," in *Wicked New Haven* (The History Press, 2013), 15–33.
21. "More of the Wakemanites," *New York Times*, January 7, 1856.
22. "State Matters," *Hartford Daily Courant*, July 3, 1865.
23. "The Seymour Town Meeting," *The Seymour Record*, October 10, 1901.

24. "Letters From the People: 'Hell Lane' vs. Orchard Street," *The Seymour Record*, July 17, 1902; "Origin of 'Hell Lane,'" *Evening Sentinel*.
25. "The Map of Seymour," *The Seymour Record*, June 26, 1902; "The New Town Maps Were Not Received," *The Seymour Record*, July 10, 1902; "The Last Book of Chronicles," *The Seymour Record*, July 17, 1902. In this latter article, the newspaper's editor opines that it was the will of a sole powerful man in town who refused to change the name on the new map and decreed, "[The road's name] shall not be changed. Hell it always was and Hell it shall always be."

12. The Summoning

1. "Connors's Ghost Story," *New York Evening World*, December 28, 1894; "Revealed by an Apparition," *Boston Journal*, December 28, 1894. Some dialogue included in this chapter has been re-created to help explain the characters' mindsets and to establish the story's setting. Otherwise, all cited quotes are taken from actual accounts found in December 1894 newspapers.
2. "An Apparition Appeared," *Cleveland Leader*, December 29, 1894.
3. "A Peculiar Coincidence," *New York Tribune*, December 28, 1894.
4. The exact time of eleven o'clock, as noted by John Connors, is recorded in every newspaper source listed here.
5. "Connors's Ghost Story."
6. "Thought His Aunt Was Ill: John Connors Walks Seven Miles in a Blinding Storm and Finds It True," *Hartford Courant*, December 28, 1894.

13. Living Apparitions: A Doppelgänger's Forewarning

1. Samuel Byron Brittan's (1815–1883) biographical information is scant. However, one excellent source concerning this fascinating individual and Spiritualism as a whole is provided by the online source, *The International Association for the Preservation of Spiritualist and Occult Periodicals.* An examination of Brittan, written during his lifetime, is also included in William Hunt's "Samuel B. Brittan," *American Biographical Sketch Book* (Nafis & Cornish, 1848), 270–71.
2. Davis discusses his life and the occult in *The Magic Staff: An Autobiography of Andrew Jackson Davis* (J.S. Brown & Co., 1857).

3. Brittan's twelve-day trance and his Penn Medical University degree are mentioned in Delight W. Dodyk, "Education and Agitation: The Woman Suffrage Movement in New Jersey" (diss., Rutgers, 1997), 550–51.
4. Information regarding inventor William Godley Creamer (1821–1898) appears in "William Godley Creamer," *Proceedings at the Nineteenth Annual Meeting and Nineteenth Annual Festival of the New England Society in the City of Brooklyn* (Brooklyn, NY, 1899), 14–15. Creamer's life is illuminated in his obituary, *Brooklyn Eagle*, April 22, 1898. According to Brittan, Creamer lived in Ansonia during the late 1840s, *Benham's New Haven Directory and Annual Advertiser 1853–54* (J.H. Benham, 1853). Brittan notes that Creamer was at one time boarding on Cherry Street in Birmingham (Derby) during 1853.
5. *The Derby Journal* (during 1847–49) offered various advertisements for "Wm. G. Creamer's" (and sometimes W.G. Creamer's) stove and metal working shop. One of these sales ads dated September 28, 1848, is for cooking and parlor stoves and notes Creamer's business address as "Naugatuck Bridge, Derby, Conn."
6. Brittan's first mention of Bailey's "living apparition" appears in "Extraordinary Psychical Phenomena," *Spiritual Telegraph*, September 23, 1854.
7. Joseph Trowbridge Bailey (1806–1854) is recognized as a Spiritualist in Emma Hardinge, *Modern American Spiritualism: A Twenty Years' Record of the Communion Between Earth and the World of Spirits* (Published by the author, 1870). Bailey's Spiritualist beliefs are stressed by Edward Fitch Bullard in his letter stating, "[Bailey]…looked into the Spirit-land with the brightest anticipations," as reprinted in the work, S.B. Brittan, ed., *The Spiritual Telegraph*, vol. 4 (Partridge & Brittan, 1854), 303. Biographical information is also gleaned from "The Death of Mr. Joseph T. Bailey," *Philadelphia Inquirer*, March 21, 1854.
8. One possible candidate concerning the mysterious "Mr. F" could be Raymond French (1805–1886), an important auger manufacturer residing in Seymour, Connecticut. On two occasions, French's factories burned to the ground: in 1841 and again in 1849. These personal disasters might explain the "dark cloud" statement both the living apparition and the real-life Joseph Trowbridge Bailey related to Samuel Brittan. Events of Raymond French's life are mentioned in W.C. Sharpe, *Seymour and Vicinity* (Record Print, 1878) and also in Campbell, Sharpe and Bassett, *Seymour, Past and Present.*
9. S.B. Brittan, *Man and His Relations: Illustrating the Influence of the Mind on the Body* (W.A. Townsend, 1864), 337.

About the Author

Award-winning author Michael J. Bielawa is dedicated to researching and celebrating the Naugatuck Valley's unique history. Well-versed with New England's supernatural heritage, his explorations of the Northeast's most mysterious and sacred sites have resulted in numerous books and articles, including *Wicked Bridgeport* (which received the first-ever "New England Paranormal Literary Award") as well as the extremely popular *Wicked New Haven*. Bielawa has presented his paranormal findings in front of world academic conferences such as the NecronomiCon in Providence, Rhode Island, and at the Northeast Popular Culture Association's gatherings at Worcester State University. His eerie essays have appeared in *The Revenant*, *The Edgar Allan Poe Review*, *Fortean Times*, *Fate* magazine, *Lovecraft Proceedings*, the *Connecticut Post* and *Connecticut Magazine*. A frequent guest on television, radio and podcasts, Bielawa has celebrated New England's strange heritage with audiences on NPR, WABC, WPLR's *Chaz & AJ in the Morning* show, WICC and on WTNH's *Good Morning Connecticut* and C*onnecticut Style*. His efforts in highlighting regional history have been featured in the *New York Times*, the *Washington Post* and the *Wall Street Journal*. Have a story to share about your own paranormal experiences? Michael Bielawa wants to hear from you. Please contact Bielawa at mbielawa@hotmail.com.